Life of a Raavulan

ALT *Life*
voices and stories

AltLife offers stories of individuals, communities and societies. Their voices bear witness to a history, a milieu, an experience, and offer new ways of seeing and understanding our times.

Life of a Raavulan

P. K. Kariyan
with Fazeela Mehar

Translated by
V. Prathiba

Orient BlackSwan

All rights reserved. No part of this book may be (i) modified, reproduced or utilised in any form, or by any means, electronic or mechanical, including photocopying, recording or by any information storage and retrieval system, in any form of binding or cover other than in which it is published, without permission in writing from the publisher; or (ii) used or reproduced in any manner for the purpose of training, development or operation of artificial intelligence (AI) technologies and systems, including generative AI technologies, without permission in writing from the copyright holder.

LIFE OF A RAAVULAN

ORIENT BLACKSWAN PRIVATE LIMITED

Registered Office
3-6-752 Himayatnagar, Hyderabad 500 029, Telangana, India
Email: centraloffice@orientblackswan.com

Other Offices
Bengaluru, Chennai, Guwahati, Hyderabad, Kolkata, Mumbai,
New Delhi, Noida, Patna

© Orient Blackswan Private Limited 2026
First published 2026

ISBN 978 93 6973 287 6

041733

Typeset in Cambria 13/15 *by*
K. Divya, Hyderabad 500 060

Printed at
Manipal Technologies Limited, Manipal

Published by
Orient Blackswan Private Limited
3-6-752, Himayatnagar,
Hyderabad 500 029, Telangana, India
Email: info@orientblackswan.com

Contents

Foreword by P. Sanal Mohan   vii
Preface   xiii
Translator's Preface   xv

1. Creation   1
2. How the Raavulas Came into Being   4
3. Amma and Maaman   9
4. My Birth and Achan's Death   14
5. My School, My Native Place, My People   19
6. Learning Becomes Serious Business   25
7. Childhood Memories   29
8. Aashramam School, and then to S.K.M.J.   35
9. The Memories of S.K.M.J.   39
10. An Unforgettable Episode   43
11. The Gods Continue Their Journey   48
12. That One Year I Skipped School   51
13. Thrissilery and Varghese   58
14. Meeting Varghese   62
15. Memories of Varghese   67
16. The Thirunelli–Thrissilery Episode   73

17.	After the Attack, Peruman's Murder	76
18.	To the Jail	80
19.	Memories of the Days Spent in Jail	84
20.	The Trial	89
21.	A Raavulan's Political Statement	95
22.	Imprisonment under MISA and the Emergency	99
23.	Freedom, and Activities Afterwards	103
24.	Work, Family	107
25.	I Start Learning about My Community	111
26.	The End of the Story of Our Origins	114
27.	Rituals and Customs of the Raavulas	116
28.	Gaddika—for Humans and Nature	120
29.	How the Raavulas became Adiyaas	122
Postscript		*125*

Foreword

'Writing lives' remains central to the narratives of indigenous communities. These narratives encompass their histories and struggle for survival, and imagine a future that would evolve through their struggles. Life, as it is lived, is an ensemble of their histories that envelop the lives of their parents and the generations past with that of the life of the present generation. Enfolded in the past, nourished by their blood and sweat, the oppressive present becomes an invitation to life, evolving through the hardship of the times. However, people make their histories through these struggles. This book is a living example of the struggles of generations of oppressed Raavulas as objectified through the life narrative of the legendary P. K. Kariyan, authored by Fazeela Mehar.

Life writing has evolved as a significant genre for oppressed peoples worldwide to articulate their histories and visions of a possible future. From life narratives of enslaved African American people from the United States and narratives of Native Americans, to the narratives of Aboriginal Australians, we have several examples that have helped broaden our understanding of the lifeworld of the oppressed. Closer home, we have the narratives of Dalit lives—those that are authored by Dalits and Adivasis and those authored by researchers and scholars. Today, such autobiographical and biographical writings have come to assume canonical status as a genre, giving rise to multiple other genres.

As a researcher, I trace the beginnings of such examples of self-writing to the nineteenth-century writings of missionaries. In these writings, one comes across fragments of the lives of the slave castes in Kerala. Similar fragmentary lives are available in Dutch colonial archival sources related to Kerala. They also appear fleetingly in the archival records related to the parliamentary papers on slavery in India. From these examples, we may formulate our arguments on the significance of life narratives as sources of history. Following this perspective, we may read *Life of A Raavulan* and journey along with the narrative's author and protagonist.

While we have a good corpus of Dalit life narratives, we are just beginning to see the emergence of life narratives of Adivasis. We probably have comparatively more historical writings on the Adivasi community of Mala Arayas in Kerala, as they came into contact with the Church Missionary Society in Travancore, as scholars like Jose Peter have argued. The small group of Kurichya Adivasis of Wayanad who accepted Catholicism in the early twentieth century also entered the regime of historical records. I also signpost the life narrative of C. K. Janu. We may also observe the colonial ethnographic writings on the Adivasis of Wayanad. In such cases, we come across fragments of the lives of the oppressed people. In this book, for example, P. K. Kariyan contests the claims of some well-known author–bureaucrats on the Adivasis of Wayanad. In contemporary life narratives, we get a different picture of the life of the oppressed as they unfold in different contexts of everyday life, engaging with the structures of power. In other words, what unfolds today is the agency of Adivasis themselves.

Life of A Raavulan opens with the origin narrative of the community, which radiates goodwill; the all-encompassing nature of their worldview dominates as the creation story unfolds. This story is sutured around the life narrative of the protagonist P. K. Kariyan, and the creation story concludes as the protagonist's story ends. The readers are tasked with imagining the parallel evolution of the contemporary life of the Adivasis and their mythical origins. The origin story concludes only at the end of the protagonist P. K. Kariyan's life narrative, as the mythical provides certain depth to the layers of meanings that the text encompasses, mainly when practices like Gaddika are discussed. As a ritual enactment, Gaddika is meant for the well-being of both nature and humans, which may indicate the flourishing of a certain synergy between the worlds of humans and non-humans.

While the mythical origin remains more in the metaphysical realm, the author and protagonist digresses to the earthly concerns. Identifying the possible migration of the Raavulans/Adiyaans to the Wayanad region of Kerala from the Karnataka region, locates them in history. There is a spatiality shared equally by the mythology and the lived history, when they identify the geographical area where they finally settle down as cultivators and labourers. That area is the land bordering the Brahmagiri ranges, known as Thrissilery. According to the author, 'It is a typical Wayanad village, guarded by the Brahmagiri hills and with acres of plain paddy fields. This is the land of so much history, so many rebellions and revolutions, and ancient epics as well as robust tribal lives.' The village's rice fields are the surface, bearing these inscriptions that a committed researcher can decipher. As the author and protagonist Kariyan narrates his life, they can observe changes everywhere, including the imposing mountain ranges; 'the only thing that doesn't change or fade away is the history of these lands'—which is to be conjured.

The matrilineal system of family lineage practised by the Raavulas gave an important role to the maternal uncle. In the life of Kariyan, his uncle P. K. Kaalan was the most influential figure, more than his parents, who appear in the narrative fleetingly. His uncle (maaman) would become a significant figure in the community and an accomplished Gaddika practitioner. The most distinctive aspect of Kariyan's life was his involvement in the Naxalite movement that, despite its failures, secured the rights of the oppressed Raavulas who were agricultural labourers working under precapitalist regimes of power. From his birth to childhood, Kariyan's life and all the experiences that made him a person with critical knowledge, emanated from his uncle's influence over him—to the extent that even as he remained an iconic figure, he would refer to himself as 'maaman's gift'.

As the author narrates the birth and childhood of Kariyan, we come across a past that has already gone beyond retrieval. However, the individuals and events of the past bring forward the life of Adivasi communities in general and Adiyaans in particular. Labouring is described intensely along with several other aspects of their everyday lives; the role of elders, both men and women, in shaping the future of the younger generation, also assumes significance in the social memory. We also get to know about food practices, and the role of elder women in raising families. It provides excellent details about the marriage practices among the Raavulas, which defined the role of men and women in the community in contrast to the practices of the dominant agricultural castes of Wayanad and Kerala.

Another critical element is the struggle for dignity and encounter with forms of untouchability as recalled in the incident at the local tea shop. We observe similar incidents in various parts of Malabar around the same time. The violent reaction of the oppressed-caste people brought about changes to such indignities.

Literacy in traditional societies has been discussed as a significant aspect of the modernisation theory. In this book, we come across a particular moment of modernisation coming through films, that demanded literacy to read the film notices distributed in the local world of advertisements. Kariyan's uncle wanted him to read out the synoptic stories of the films in the notices, and therefore, he wanted Kariyan to go to school. We come across Kariyan's struggles in school and also his success, although he does not go for tertiary education. Eventually, his uncle also learns to read. Kariyan also refers to his teachers who remained as pathfinders for him. We also learn about his encounters with the question of social identity while at school.

The politics in which the community is embedded becomes apparent in the analysis of the everyday labour of the people in the fields of upper-caste landlords. A reprieve in the situation comes when they go to work for the migrant Christian peasants. In this larger context, the communist party enters the picture, demanding legitimate wages and dignified working conditions. Subsequently, the same people behind the party organisation become Naxalites; Varghese, the legendary leader, becomes part of the life and struggles of the Raavulas who think of him to be their 'Peruman', more than a leader of the community. The dignified position of Peruman, ascribed to Varghese, represents the intimate chord between Varghese and the Raavulas. More importantly, unlike other upper-caste leaders, Varghese becomes the most trusted communist enshrined in the people's hearts as he identifies himself completely with the community. After the Naxalite action at Pulpally in Wayanad, for two years, he is able to hide out among the community, without being arrested; he is a real revolutionary who lived with the people like fish in water, as Kariyan recalls later.

After the killing of Varghese, all those who were suspected to be Naxalites were arrested, and thus, Kariyan ended up in jail. As he recalls, he became a Naxalite after he was falsely implicated. In other words, as narrated in the text, the reading and learning while in jail made him a learned revolutionary, the spirit of which he carried to the last moment of his life. He never thought bloodshed would change a society or bring in a revolution. Like in the case of many revolutionaries in jail, the jail library was the real university for him. Parallels can be read in the narratives of jail life by great figures like Malcolm X.

Kariyan became an iconic figure through his learning and critical reflection. He showed the Raavulas a new path, combining radical politics and community ethos, which provided the ethical ground for his political practice. It is a life meant not just for the Raavulas but for the whole of Kerala and India, where oppression continues in several forms, even today. Fazeela Mehar has done an important work by narrating Kariyan's life in the larger political and social context, which has the power to humanise the realms of politics and culture in our contemporary times beset with fascist threats.

P. Sanal Mohan

Preface

It was the year 2018. My path to P. K. Kariyan and his life story began in the wake of three interviews I had done for the *Madhyamam* weekly, marking the fiftieth anniversary of the Naxalite action in Pulpally and Thalassery. What prompted me was an urge to look beyond the oft-repeated tales of Naxalism in Kerala, particularly in Wayanad, and to gain an insight into the lesser-known stories in connection with the movement. I wanted to find the 'ordinary' people, the unsung heroes, who had quietly carried those histories within them. Of course, it arose from my curiosity, but there was also an urge to bring lives and memories out of the shadows before silence claimed them forever.

My journey began with one-on-one conversations with P. K. Kariyan. As he shared his unfiltered thoughts, they profoundly influenced not only my work but also my very being. His narration of his personal story was to open a door into the struggles of an entire community. It was indeed a classic example of the personal becoming political. This is just a beginning—an invitation to continue, to gather more stories, to preserve cultural traces and alternative voices of history that might otherwise be lost as part of our historical/cultural amnesia.

With that same spirit of expectation, I welcome the English edition of P. K. Kariyan's life writing, first brought to readers in Malayalam by Mathrubhumi Books. I am grateful to Orient BlackSwan for bringing this work to a wider readership. I remember with gratitude Sreenath Sreedharan, Assistant Publisher (Humanities), whose support made this endeavour possible. My thanks, with warmth and admiration, to the translator, V. Prathiba. My respect and gratitude also go to P. Sanal Mohan, who, despite his many commitments, graciously found the time to write the Foreword for this book.

And finally, with no need for formality, I offer my deepest gratitude to that extraordinary human being, P. K. Kariyan, for entrusting me with his life and voice, and for allowing his story to become part of mine.

Fazeela Mehar

Translator's Preface

History is not a mere collection of information and chronology. Its purpose extends well beyond storytelling, says Romila Thapar in *Our History, Their History, Whose History?*. Thapar recognises nationalism as a powerful force that generates narratives providing communities with ancestries and shaping the course of societies. Looked at from this angle, *Life of A Raavulan* is a narrative that provides an ancestry to the Raavula community. It is a life history presented in the form of an autobiography. Kariyan presents an Adivasi history through the oral narrative of his life and times to Fazeela Mehar, a journalist and writer. She in turn captures the very cadence of Kariyan's narration, in writing, without losing the tenor and tone of his speech. The Malayalam edition—*Oru Raavulante Jeevitha Pusthakam*—was published in March 2023, by Mathrubhumi Books.

The Adivasi histories that Kariyan narrates are the living experiences of a vibrant culture. The significance of this work lies in that Kariyan—from the Raavula tribe—offers a first-hand account of the centuries-long history and resistance of the Raavulas. What emerges from this is a new history of those who are subordinated, ignored, overlooked and relegated to the margins of sociopolitical processes—a history of those who are unrepresented in the state archives. This is an attempt to 'write' the Raavulas into the annals of history. The thick walls of denial by the mainstream are thus pierced through. This work is a discourse attending to the ethnography and sociopolitical history of the Raavulas.

Adivasi literature is unique in its communitarian, resistant, and outspoken nature, rooted in shared aesthetic values. It is eco-friendly, pastoral, mystical, non-dualistic, and spiritual, with a strong mythical consciousness. Their writings are their own voices describing their lives, cultures, world views and religion. To make themselves heard, they had to overcome the dynamics of exclusion. Marginalised minorities often form the deepest pockets of inequity. Discrimination and stereotyping lower their self-esteem. These Adivasis are among India's most marginalised socio-economic groups. Displacement, erosion of distinct cultures and identities, loss of traditional livelihoods, exploitation, marginalisation, lack of education and healthcare, poverty, and unemployment have made them the poorest and most vulnerable section of society. They face a deep crisis of identity and existence due to the lack of means of communication. They have long been denied their citizenly voice, and restoring that voice is the need of the hour.

What sparked my interest in undertaking and presenting an English translation of Fazeela's Malayalam work was the sense of a cultural odyssey that unfolds as Kariyan narrates the rich tapestry of Raavula life, weaving together stories of heritage, wisdom and resilience. He recounts his experiences, struggles and insights as an Adivasi navigating a changing world. His narration is deeply rooted in oral traditions—songs and stories passed down through generations. The unique worldview of an Adivasi community is revealed here. Kariyan's work invites you to listen to a cultural heritage that transcends time, fostering a deeper understanding of indigenous perspectives. It is an invitation to explore the richness of the Raavula culture. Lively, informative and insightful, this work is groundbreaking not only as literature but also as history. This translation is meant to introduce to the readers the fascinating and diverse world of the Raavulas. It is also a tribute to the courage and wisdom of Kariyan, who had overcome many difficulties and hardships to become a respected leader of his community, a 'Mooppan', a renowned Gaddika artist, and a source of inspiration to his people.

Readers may come to a translation with their own preconceived and often unrealistic perceptions, or little knowledge of the source culture and lifestyle. Translators are in a unique position to act as ambassadors between cultures. I felt that this unique work, interweaving several discourses, needs to reach a wider audience. It opens up for the reader a rich tapestry of Adivasi life. Adivasi literature hardly receives pan-Indian recognition and attention, unless it is translated into an accessible language. There is an urgent need to bring such narratives to a wider audience, in order to protect Adivasi identities and existence in the face of intensified exploitation.

The narrative explains in detail how dire their economic and social conditions were; how they were deprived of basic necessities such as food, clothing, healthcare, education and employment; how they were subjected to humiliation; and how development plans never reached their rightful beneficiaries. Kariyan narrates his life from childhood to adulthood, sharing his experiences, struggles and insights at each stage. He reflects on the history, tradition and culture of his tribe. This is a first-hand narration of the Raavula people's history, detailing their initial compliance, subsequent resistance, and life across centuries. The idea that the personal is political is central to this narrative. A strong sense of community and a sense of collectivity help the Adivasis to rise above the narrow walls of individualism. This unity and selflessness or altruism are valued traits in their culture as opposed to the 'me-alone' trait celebrated in the individualistic culture of the so-called sophisticated 'mainstream'.

Kariyan's strongest source of influence and role model was his uncle (maaman) Kaalan. Kariyan was the first generation in his family to become literate, thanks to his uncle. His uncle was determined to provide him with a good education against all odds and cared deeply about his intellectual growth. The book speaks at length about

Kariyan's educational opportunities and his attitude towards it. His enthusiasm for formal education and school life seems to fluctuate as per the situations he is presented with. Kariyan became one of the earliest Adivasi prisoners in Kerala. His arrest takes place during a school vacation, though he has not committed any wrong. His education comes to a complete halt when he is branded a Naxalite and imprisoned for five and a half years.

Kariyan also speaks of an era of political turbulence in Kerala. He engages with the historic moments connected with the Naxal movement in Kerala, from an intensely personal point of view that is not divorced from the lived realities of the time. The arrival of the Naxal movement in Kerala was part of the larger Maoist insurgency taking place in various parts of India. The Naxals wanted to overthrow the existing social order. In Wayanad, they tried to mobilise Adivasi communities and plantation workers against the terrible injustices meted out to them. It left a lasting impact on the history, politics and culture of Kerala. Later on, it inspired writers, artists and activists to explore themes of oppression, resistance and injustice. When Kariyan speaks of the movement, we see perspectives that are absent from history books written from the mainstream point of view. For Kariyan, it was Comrade Varghese who first awakened an awareness of their Adivasi rights among the community. His narration provides a haunting reminder of the injustices inflicted upon the Adivasis by landlords. Varghese, who became 'Peruman' for the Adivasis, along with other Naxal activists, fought against the ill treatment and exploitation of the illiterate Adivasis of Wayanad in the 1960s.

The media reports detailing Naxal attacks often intimidated us with their narratives of blood-curdling incidents of attacks on landlords. They painted Varghese and his comrades in a nightmarish and cruel light for the rest of Kerala. But Kariyan had total adoration for Varghese.

He is eloquent about the humane aspects of Varghese's character. There were many more like Kariyan among the Adivasis who mourned the death of their hero, Varghese.

The Adivasi identity is intrinsically and symbiotically connected to nature, rituals and cultural practices. Kariyan addresses the question of how the Adivasi name 'Raavula' was changed to 'Adiyaas'. He says that it is not just a quirky change in nomenclature but a cultural annihilation. Adivasis are identified by their ethnic names. To give them another name amounts to imposing another identity on them. And the imposed new name/identity is quite different from what they perceive themselves to be.

Kariyan provides a long account of his prison life and legal struggles in various courts of law. His warm relationship with his uncle also takes up many pages in the book. As the narrative moves ahead, it reveals a change in Kariyan's attitude—from that of an uncommitted youngster to one engrossed in social commitments and political activities.

Kariyan refutes the books written by mainstream non-Adivasi writers about Adivasi life and society. Instead, he outlines an alternative history. Kariyan's life story itself is a comprehensive reference work on the social and cultural life of the Raavula community—which if unwritten could have otherwise been lost to the posterity. Similarly, the Adivasi art form Gaddika could have been lost, if not followed up by artists like Kariyan, in the face of overwhelming clamour by those who did not want to keep it alive.

Life of A Raavulan is a rich repository of knowledge on the specific historical, cultural and geographical location where the Raavulas have lived for centuries. It narrates processes that are at the core of 'being a Raavula', their cultural specificities, values and beliefs, ways of life and worldviews. They live in their own egalitarian society, all in solidarity with one another—one for all and all for one. The strong sense of community and collectivity helps them to rise above the narrow walls of individualism. They have their own values and ethos, their own myths and legends. They have their own notions about present life and life after death. Their sense of social responsibility is such that they find happiness and gratification in sharing and not hoarding. The narrative also touches upon lives of other Adivasi groups in Wayanad, who face similar threats of losing their identity and agency.

I have tried to preserve the authenticity and richness of Kariyan's voice, brought to us through Fazeela's narrative. But at the same time, I would like to stress the fact that every telling is a retelling. There is always this demand for translation to perfectly reproduce the 'original' source text. And translation is either expected to perform the miracle of perfect reproduction, or dismissed out of hand as treacherous and fraudulent. The circulation of literature across the world is inevitably tied to translation. As a text crosses cultural and linguistic boundaries, so too do the interpretations of its content. Let us also remember that translation is the most intimate form of reading. It is an act that seeks to reimagine the text.

I am glad to make this unique work accessible to both the English-speaking world and a pan-Indian readership, especially when there is an urgent need for circulating and hearing a plurality of voices across the globe. I sincerely hope that this work will not only inform and educate readers, but also challenge them to think critically and empathetically about the issues and realities of Adivasi communities across India and beyond. Hopefully, it would also foster a dialogue and solidarity around Adivasi rights and dignity. I also hope that it would do justice to the source text in reflecting Kariyan's vision and voice, as well as inspire an understanding and appreciation of Kerala's diverse Adivasi culture.

V. Prathiba

1
Creation

In the beginning, there was only the sky and the earth. In the sky, the moon appeared first, followed by the sun. Then came countless gods and goddesses. Only afterwards did humankind come into being.

That's our belief. When we say the moon appeared first in the sky, we do suppose that initially it was dark or night, followed by light or day. Thus it's the moon who gives light in the pervading darkness. It was only after this that the sunrise and daytime came into existence. Therefore, as per our belief, we give priority to the moon.

Among the gods and goddesses, the most important were Aariyan and Baaniyan. Once, when the innumerable gods were seated in the courtyard of their heavenly abode, lost in deep thought, a sudden realisation dawned upon them: What is the purpose of our existence alone? Who is there to worship us, to sustain us with devotion, and to honor us with ceremonial offerings?

As they thought long and hard, they found an answer to their worries. It was to create 'human beings' who resembled them. Their thoughts thus led to the creation of human beings—and to the genesis of the Raavulas.

***

2 Life of A Raavulan

Kariyan Mooppan (1951–2020)

We Raavulas, like other tribal communities, have many songs of our own. These songs are chanted or sung during our rituals and poojas and gatherings. These songs are like the living breath to us. These songs, which emanate from our very being, give solace to our body and mind. They include wedding songs, Gaddika songs, Vellattu songs,

Thera songs, Peyattu songs (Kooliyattam) and Chembene songs, among others. There are lots of them which we sing during the Valiya Pela,[1] for amusement—songs which have elements of both fun and facts. All these songs do have much deeper meanings too. These songs in fact narrate our lives. They speak of where we came from, how we live, where we are bound to, who our gods are, what we can achieve with the help of these gods, what is impossible to achieve, how we confront death when it happens to one from the community. . . . And the words of these songs have many meanings.

If we trace the genesis of the Raavulas, we need to go through the Pulapattu (Pula song). But even in the Pulapattu, one can see that the original has gone through many transformations over the years. Not just that, there are differences in songs and legends depending on the places where the Raavula communities have lived and settled. The stories are not the same in Thrissilery and Thirunelli or Pakkanadu (Bavali)[2]. Although they sound the same, there are differences in forms and patterns. There is no single evolution myth or story among tribals, unlike in the case of religions. For us, *desham*[3] is very important. It is at the same time minute as well as expansive. Though for the outsiders, our world might appear small and insignificant, in fact our original world is much bigger, many times bigger, than the non-tribal world.

We can start my story from this juncture—from the question of how we Raavulas came into being, we can move on to the question of how I came into being.

---

[1] Valiya Pela is the final rite among the post-death rituals of the Raavulas. The impurity associated with a death in the family is considered completely removed only after this ritual is performed. Once it is concluded, the family is freed from 'pela'.
[2] Villages in the Wayanad district
[3] Place of dwelling

2
How the Raavulas Came into Being

The first challenge the gods faced was deciding what to name their new creation. After much deliberation, they reached a consensus: the new being would be called 'Human Being' (*Manushyan*). The next issue they faced was what material should be used to fashion human beings. After a few rounds of discussions, they found an answer for that too. To create human beings in the most natural manner, the gods decided soil was the best material. But still, that was not the end of their problems. What kind of soil was best for creation? If human beings were to be fashioned from soil mixed with gravel and stones, it would be impossible to shape them into a form of beauty. So, they needed to find soil which was not mixed with gravel. What kind of soil could be so pure? The gods tested all kinds of soil. Finally, they concluded that the soil found in termite mounds was the best.

When we understand that gods chose soil from termite mounds for the creation of human beings, we can definitely assume that they had made termite mounds and termites much before the creation of human beings. Unless there are termites, there won't be termite mounds. So, we can assume that the gods had created other living beings as well as natural vegetation long before the creation of human beings. But this is not mentioned in the Raavulas' *Song of Genesis*.

So finally everything was decided. Now the gods had to find the termite mounds for the creation. They went to the king of termites. They had their bows and arrows with them. They asked the king of termites to provide some soil out of the mounds. The termite king asked them, 'Why do you want our soil?' The gods replied that it was to be used for the creation of human beings and added that in future, his people would benefit from these humans. The termite king agreed to provide soil from the mounds. But he said, 'I can give you the soil on one condition. I have to first take a bath and purify myself. In the meantime, you all please wait here.' The gods agreed and the termite king went for a bath.

The gods took this opportunity to steal and hide as much soil as they could—beneath the nails of fingers and toes, on the edges of their bowstrings, and on the edge where the arrow is put on the bow. When the termite king returned from his bath, he measured the soil and found that it was less than what he had left behind.

He asked the gods, 'Did you steal my soil?'

The gods said, 'No!' and added, 'When we re-measure an already measured thing, it is bound to be a little less.'

The termite king was not convinced. He still suspected them. The gods asked him, 'Are you trying to say we are thieves?'

Then the gods found a way to cover up their robbery. They said, 'Let us take a bath in the flowing river.' And they put forward a condition to the termite king. 'You should take a bath on the north side of the river and we gods will take our bath on the south. If at all we have stolen the soil, water mixed with soil will flow towards the northern side.'

The termite king didn't realise the treachery in this. So he agreed and both the gods and the king got into the river, as decided. Naturally, the soil hidden by the gods mixed with water and flowed further south. The king had no answer. He could now no longer persist with the allegation that the gods had stolen the soil. Thus, the termite king gave soil from the mound to the gods who returned to heaven with it.

Once they reached heaven, the gods kneaded the soil and got ready for creation. Then they had another doubt. They thought they could create women in the resemblance of their own mothers. What form could they give to the men? Then they found a way to solve the problem: they decided to look at each other and start sculpting the men. Thus, they created human beings and gave life to these creations.

And yet problems remained. The new issue was that the new creations could not talk or walk. The gods were disappointed, thinking that all their work until now had come to nothing. The disappointed and sad gods decided to go on a journey to find a solution to their new problem. They crossed hills, mountains, forests and valleys on their journey....

***

In order to reach Thrissilery, one has to cross the forest and climb down a hill. Thrissilery Naadu is the 'land' of the Raavulas. We don't go by the borders drawn by the Panchayath or the village. We have a different concept of our land. For us it is Thrissilery Naadu, extending from Anamala stream to Vannathikolli, and from Paambanmotta to Thanneerpanthal. We Raavulas lived within these boundaries. This is my own land, where I was born. As per Panchayat records, the place is known by the name Thrissilery, whereas for us Raavulas it is 'Thrissilery Naadu'.

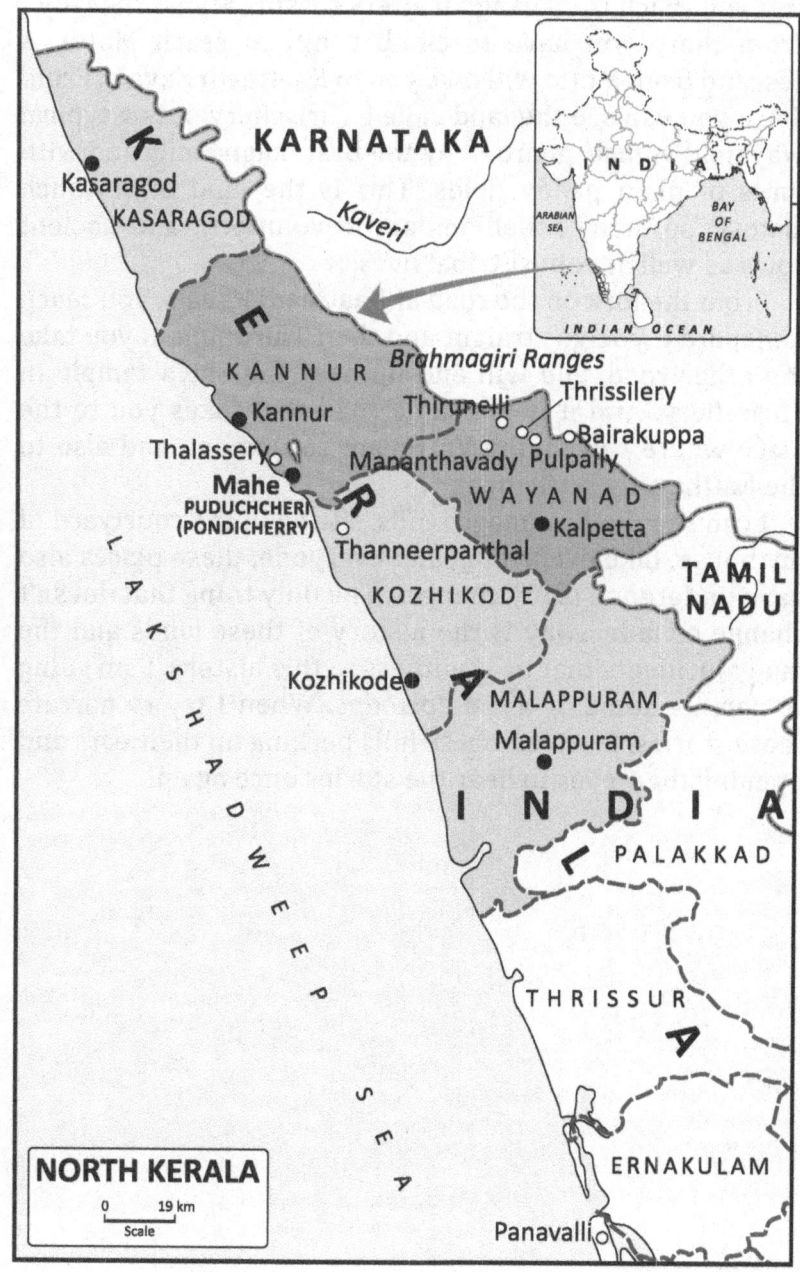

You will reach Ondayangadi after crossing Mananthavady.[1] From there you have to climb a hill to reach Motta. A descend from Motta will take you to Kaattaadi Kavala. From there you can see the land called Thrissilery. It is a typical Wayanad village, guarded by the Brahmagiri hills and with acres of plain paddy fields. This is the land of so much history, so many rebellions and revolutions, and ancient epics as well as robust tribal lives.

From the fork on the road at Kaattaadi Kavala, you reach Aanapara if you go straight and then Thirunelli. If you take the other road, you will end up near the Shiva temple in Thrissilery. And it is the same road that takes you to the place where I lived, the Varinilam settlement, and also to the Kaithavally settlement.

I can see the Brahmagiri hills, sitting in the courtyard of my house. Like everything and everyone, these places also have undergone many changes. The only thing that doesn't change or fade away is the history of these lands and the many incidents that bear witness to this history. I am going to narrate some of these episodes. When I try to narrate these stories, I can feel these hills perking up their ears and opening their eyes to hear the stories once again.

---

[1] Places in Wayanad (see map on page 7)

3

Amma and Maaman[1]

The story of my life should begin with the story of my maaman's life. This physique of mine is my maaman's gift. P. K. Kariyan is here sitting in front of you trying to tell you his life story, only because his uncle P. K. Kaalan lived before him.

Maaman went through a lot of difficulties in life for the sake of our community and for the sake of our land. If maaman had not been here, our tribal art, Gaddika, would not have reached the public. Also, the Raavulas would not have had much visibility on the cultural map of Kerala. I have just followed maaman, even in whatever I have contributed to our community.

We are a matrilineal community, with our rights coming from our mother's side. Therefore, maaman's place in my life is all the more significant. Not just that, in my case, I was practically brought up by maaman. That had to do with the circumstances of our life.

My grandfather was Kolumban and my grandmother was called Karutha. They had a total of eleven children. However, only three survived—amma, maaman and my mother's elder sister Kaali. Amma was named Chunda. All the other siblings succumbed to some fatal illness or

---

[1] mother and uncle

the other while very young. Even maaman was not really healthy at the time of his birth. But he could be saved; and there is a story about how that happened.

My grandfather had an elder brother named Chokran. He was the Naattu Mooppan.[2] When he came to see the infant, my grandmother was crying with the baby in her lap. The situation looked grave.

Chokran looked at the baby and said, 'He will not die. I will not let him die. But if he is rescued from death, he has to be named Kaalan.'

My grandmother immediately agreed.

In those days, the whole area was forested. Chokran went into the forest, plucked a few medicinal plants, ground those leaves, and extracted the juice. This juice was poured into the mouth of the ailing baby. Chokran then went home. When he returned in the evening, the baby was playful, shaking his limbs.

'That medicine is so powerful. Like you agreed earlier, the child has to be named Kaalan,' Chokran grandfather said.

My grandfather and grandmother kept their word and named the child Kaalan. The full name was Kaalappan, which later became Kaalan.

Kaalan is also the name of our tribal god. That is why Chokran insisted on that name. Everyone said my uncle was cured because he was named after a god. But when I heard this, I felt it was the indigenous medicine, given by Chokran, that cured the ailing baby; nothing else. Those days they had their indigenous herbal medicines, the know-how to administer it, and because of the power of the medicine, the child could be saved. And it was only to make the people believe in god that Chokran asked the child to be named Kaalan. Whatever the truth, that is the story of maaman's birth.

---

[2] Tribal chief

Amma's elder sister got married and when she went to her husband's place, only amma and maaman were left to take care of our house. As my grandfather became old and could not shoulder the entire responsibility of the household, maaman too had started working. In those days, workers never got wages for their labour. So even if many people from the same household went out for work, it made little difference. Amma remained at home looking after all the household chores.

When amma reached puberty, marriage proposals started coming for her. Those days my grandfather's family lived in a place called Plamoola. It is near Thrissilery. That was our homestead. Many people came from the Thrissilery side with proposals for amma. But she was not happy with any of the proposals. She refused to meet them. Amma used to run away from the house whenever she sensed people coming with marriage proposals. No one said much about this in the early days. But as this went on, amma's behaviour led to quarrels. Brother and sister started picking on each other on the question of why she did not like any of the proposals. Maaman was three years younger to my mother. They were very close to each other. So the rest of the family, who were also fed up with amma's behaviour, left it to maaman to deal with.

In those days, girls used to get married at the age of fourteen or fifteen. So amma, who was of marriageable age, could not be left to stay on at home; it became mandatory for her to get married. Maaman used to advise her. 'It is not good that you remain in this house like this. You have to get married. All other girls in the community of your age are married.' This conversation, which would begin as a mild argument, would invariably end up in a big quarrel. In the showdown between the siblings, all the clay vessels at home would be smashed.

This was the everyday situation at home, when my achan[3] Kuruman came along with a proposal from Edappadi in Ondayangadi. Earlier, one of the tribal chiefs from the Edappadi area had come to meet our chief here and happened to see my mother. Our chief, of course, was none other than Chokran.

The chief from Edappadi asked, 'Are you ready to give this girl to me?'

Chokran said, 'I can do so only if she agrees to the proposal. I am not sure if she will be ready to go so far away.'

Then they asked my grandmother. All the elders with whom this idea was discussed, had only one thing to say: 'You have to seek consent from the girl. We are not in a position to compel her.'

Finally, the chief asked amma directly if she was willing to get married. He asked her consent but she remained silent. She went out to the courtyard silently. Even then, the proposal was being talked about between the two tribal heads with the bridegroom nowhere in sight.

Amma shared her worries with maaman. Her question was, 'How can I say yes to the proposal without seeing the bridegroom?' This response from my mother gave some hope to maaman. He guessed that amma was inclined to accept this proposal since usually she wouldn't even agree to see the bridegroom. But this time she was asking to see the groom—so that was a positive sign. Maaman went to my grandmother and talked to her about my mother's demand. So it was decided that the groom and his party would come over with an official proposal.

Only that night, after all this had been discussed and decided upon, did they learn that the groom had already been married and this was his second marriage. His first wife was no more; he had a girl child from the first marriage and he was getting married again in order to have someone

---
[3] father

to look after the child. Since he could not say yes to any proposals from his neighbourhood and his hometown, he had decided to seek a bride from the neighbouring village. However, even when amma came to know of all this, there was no change in her attitude. Hence it was decided that they would meet the groom's people, despite his background. The very next day, the chief came to see amma with the groom, my achan. The marriage was agreed upon by both parties.

4

My Birth and Achan's Death

In those days, wedding ceremonies involved a lot of formalities. If the groom said yes after seeing the girl, his sisters had to come next and approve. They would tie a special *thaali* (*mangalsutra*) on the girl if they agreed to take her as their brother's wife. Once this was done, it was customary for the groom to look after all the day-to-day expenses in the bride's house until the date of the wedding. Sometimes it could take a year or so for the wedding to take place, and till such time the groom had to meet all the expenses. He had to buy and send every household item. During this period, he had the right to go to the bride's house, have food with the family and talk to the bride. But any relations other than that were strictly banned.

Thus, achan used to come from Edappadi after the day's work. He would carry a bundle of firewood on his head and walk all the way, though Edappadi was quite a distance from my hometown. Maaman felt bad seeing the groom carrying bundles of wood day after day. Carrying a bundle of firewood was not as easy as bringing provisions to the house. So maaman declined. Achan, however, insisted that this was one of our customs, and he was afraid if he stopped bringing firewood, the wedding wouldn't take place. Maaman then asked my grandfather and grandmother to intervene to put an end to the firewood deliveries.

Such rituals were followed by everyone, sometimes for up to a year. This was a measure to see if the boy had the means to look after the girl. To marry, one had to face such obstacles. But nowadays the situation is totally different. It has changed a lot.

On the other hand, amma, too, used to visit achan's house even before their wedding. Just like the groom had the permission to come to the girl's home, so also the girl could go to the groom's house. Amma met and became quite friendly with achan's daughter from his first marriage. My chechi[1] was called Manri.

One day amma brought chechi to Plamoola, and chechi remained there till the wedding. My mother took care of chechi who was barely six months old then.

Amma liked living in Edappadi, mainly because of Thera[2] performances. And since the performances were held very near achan's house, amma could easily go and watch them. Another reason was that achan's family was comparatively well-off. They had some fields of their own, and life was comfortable. Thus, finally the wedding took place.

Maaman felt sad and started missing my mother once she went to her in-laws' house after the wedding. He couldn't bear living without seeing her. They were very close to each other. So, my uncle also went to Edappadi. He began tending cattle that belonged to a Pattar.[3]

I was born in 1951. When I was born everyone was happy, as is natural in all homes. In those days nobody would announce if it was a boy or a girl. Those who came to visit the mother and baby could, however, figure it out, since a small cradle was hung outside the main door if it

---

[1] Elder sister
[2] A ritual performance where the performer is considered to be possessed by God, rather than embodying God directly.
[3] Member of a Hindu Brahmin community, specifically Kerala Iyers or Pattars, residing in the Kerala region.

was a girl, or a tiny bow and arrow if it was a boy. This was done as soon as the child was born.

The other rituals associated with childbirth were carried out on the twenty-eighth day after the birth. On that day, the child was named and a black string tied around its waist. It was customary to invite the village chief and people from the mother's village for this ceremony. I had a silver waist chain tied around me on that day. I remember maaman telling me about the event—that many people had been invited and served good food. Even before I was six months old, my ears were pierced and I was made to wear studs. My ear studs were made of pure gold. My father had gone to the goldsmith's place and supervised the making of those studs himself. The studs remained with me even when I grew up. Then I felt ashamed and awkward walking about wearing them and took them off. Later on, someone stole them.

The fuss and attention over me while chechi was being ignored, upset amma. She had a quarrel with my father about this, and then ear studs were bought for my sister, too. Chechi had them on her ears till the day of her death. Since we were almost the same age, we were very close to each other.

Maaman stayed with us at this time. This was a sore issue with my grandfather and grandmother. They were waiting for the day maaman would return to them. But my bachelor uncle remained in Edappadi and showed no signs of going back to Plamoola.

Achan died when I was six months old. He just left us one day. On the day achan passed away, maaman had taken the cattle to the hills. The owner of the cattle started scolding him when the cattle hadn't come back, and achan asked maaman to sit at home and went in search of the missing cattle. By the time he found the cattle and took them home, he was very tired. He started vomiting and had dysentery. He went to sleep and was no more the next day. People said he must have been possessed when he went up the hill late in the evening. I don't know. I cannot even recall his face. I was too young to have any memories of him.

And all the rituals connected with death followed. Amma was strictly prohibited from stepping out of the house for one year. There was a Valiya Pela, which is also called a 'Koottam'. Until it was over, amma had to follow the rules and be tethered to the house. She should not take bath, apply oil, or talk to neighbours, or anyone for that matter. The elders of our community made sure these strictures were followed. In the midst of all these, she also had to care for my sister and me. She was completely drained.

Unable to bear all this, maaman returned to Plamoola. He gave up grazing cattle and took up other jobs. But then he could not stand being separated from my mother. So one fine day, maaman just came back to Edappadi to be with my mother.

One day he told amma, 'You must be finding it difficult to look after two infants. And you can't go out either. If this child (indicating me) is left alone like this, he will soon die. So let me take him back with me (to Plamoola).'

He assured my mother that he would take care of me. I was being breastfed at that time and amma refused the offer, saying she would manage to look after me on her own. Maaman didn't ask anyone after that and didn't broach the subject again. But one day he just returned to Plamoola, taking me along with him. When he reached home, he got an earful from my grandfather and grandmother. How, they asked, was he going to bring me up without milk? But maaman had already found a way.

There was a Warrier[4] who lived near our home and he had cows. But the members of the household could not milk the cows. And though it was unthinkable for them to

---

[4] a community within the Ambalavasi group of castes, traditionally associated with managing the temple

be in the vicinity of the untouchable Adivasis, there were no taboos on drinking the milk after we had milked the cows.

It was maaman who used to milk the Warrier's cows. After bringing me with him to Plamoola, maaman started taking a small vessel from home whenever he went to milk the cows. When milking was done, he would steal a little milk in this vessel, and bring it home for me. He brought me up on this stolen cow milk.

After one year, when the rituals of the pela were over, amma, too, came to Plamoola. There was nothing left for her in her husband's house. She brought chechi too. After a few months, there was a marriage proposal for my mother. When everyone compelled her to consent to the second marriage, she gave in. Her new husband was from Plamoola. After her wedding, they went to a place called Kulirmavu. In that married life, amma gave birth to five children. From among the five, only one is alive now. But no one knows his whereabouts.

When amma moved away after her second marriage, chechi went back to Edappadi to stay with achan's relatives. I stayed back with maaman. I didn't go with my mother. If I had accompanied her, my stepfather would not have liked it. Maaman also realised that and didn't send me to my mother. From then on, if amma wanted to see me, she had to come to our place. I started disliking amma's visits. I felt a distance from her once she got remarried. I felt she was in no way related to me. Everyone said I was jealous of my mother being taken care of by another man. Even if people forced me to sit on amma's lap, I would just get up and run away. Once I started feeling estranged from my mother, maaman became everything to me. He was both my shelter and my protector.

5

My School, My Native Place, My People

Maaman was crazy about movies and watched every film he could. He always went for the second show, walking all the way to Mananthavady and back afterward. Whether he had company or not, he would never travel any other way—only on foot. In those days there was only one theatre, called Lakshmi Talkies. There was a Warrier called Appunni who was a close friend of maaman. Both were of the same age. These two used to go for movies together at night. If it was harvesting time, one had to guard the fields. If left unguarded, pigs and thieves would take the crop. But if maaman and the Warrier were entrusted with keeping watch, they would go to the field, light a fire, sing a couple of songs and then vanish, only to return at dawn. This used to be their regular routine.

And it was maaman's love of movies that got me into school. In those days, notices or handbills were distributed announcing new movies. The notice would have a part of the movie's plot printed on it, and would ask the reader to go and watch the rest of the story on the silver screen. Neither maaman nor the Warrier knew how to read or write. There was no one around who could read the movie notices to them. Maaman, crazy about movies, badly wanted to read the notices and learn about the plots. That was how I was sent to school. My uncle reasoned that if I learnt to read and write, I could read out the cinema notices and he wouldn't have to beg someone else to read it for him. Thus, I was put in school. The school was in Thrissilery and had only one teacher. Along with me a few other children from our community had also joined school.

The school came into being after the arrival of the migrant *kudiettakkaru*.[1] Their arrival transformed our area. The school building was built with the cooperation of all, in a voluntary effort. Those days there was a lot of free land available. There were no demarcations by the revenue or forest department. The landlords would just look at a stretch of land and declare the land to be theirs. When the immigrants came, they began to take over these lands, and made it their own through agriculture. The threats from landlords had no effect on them. The landlords were able to threaten only the tribals like us. The immigrants on the other hand found suitable land and made them their own.

Ironically, even the landlords had once been immigrants. They had moved in when the temples of Thrissilery, Thirunelli and Valliyoorkkavu were built. Maybe they had immigrated along with Pazhassi.[2] When our grandfathers spoke of the old days, they used to tell us about all these migrations and point out that all these people had come in only very recently. These people settled in the area around the temple. They couldn't be found anywhere other than near the temples. All the rest of the land was occupied by our people.

---

[1] Non-tribals from other parts of Kerala who migrated to tribal lands and forest areas, in search of land and livelihood

[2] Pazhassi Raja, also known as Kerala Varma Pazhassi Raja, was an important warrior from the Kottayam royal family. He is known for resisting the British East India Company's efforts to take over North Kerala in the late eighteenth and early nineteenth centuries. He waged a guerilla war against the British with the help of tribals. He was killed in a battle near Pulpally in Wayanad.

In the early days, no one from our community would work in the land belonging to these *kudiettakkaru*. But later on, they started going to work there too. The landlords had warned us that these immigrants were cannibals and that they would eat us up. The landlords had asked us to have nothing to do with the immigrants. So we used to hide from them. But nothing of the sort would happen on our school campus. All of us, be it the immigrants or the tribals, used to play together. We were just kids. How are we to know about all these taboos? There were kids from the landlords' houses also in the school. Until then, their children had their education in the Mananthavady Board School. When the new school came up in our vicinity, they all shifted there.

The children of the landlords used to talk to us and play with us in school. Once they reached their homes, they acted in a different manner. Once out of the school compound, we could not step into their houses or approach them. We were not allowed to even touch them. When we were within the school premises or on the way to school, there were no such problems at all. We were small kids. We were not contaminated by thoughts of caste or untouchability. If they wanted to pluck a mango, they needed our help. In those days our place had lots of gooseberries. We used to climb up trees to get gooseberries for them. They were not capable of physical activities like climbing trees. They only knew how to eat the mangoes and gooseberries we plucked for them. We were used to walking across hills and mountains, used to working hard. So, they could not do without us.

Among the immigrants, the majority were Christians. We were warned and threatened to not mix with the immigrant children. These children used to bring boiled tapioca to school. That was the first time we saw tapioca in our life. Before that, we hadn't seen it, we hadn't eaten it, and we hadn't even heard of tapioca. Tapioca was brought into our lives by the immigrants.

We were warned by the landlords that if we ate tapioca, we would die. So we didn't eat it at all. Those days we couldn't think of asking: how come the immigrant children were still alive after eating tapioca? But inside the school compound, it was a different story. We would eat the tapioca they brought along, with green chili paste on the side. We wouldn't talk about this at home. They also used to eat what we brought from our homes. We all used to eat together at school. There was no differentiation at all, even among the Warriers and Brahmins. But once we got ready to go back home from school, they used to tell us not to speak about this at home. If the people at home got to know about it, they would literally flay us as well as them. They were told that once touched by an Adivasi child, they were good for nothing.

During the month of *kanni*,[3] there was always a shortage of food, and it was during this time that people in our community began eating tapioca. We couldn't find any work during this month. It was then that we started going to the immigrants for work. We would be served tapioca and we ate it. We also started bringing some tapioca back home after work. Thus it became a part of our diet. In those days, our staple foods included rice, ragi and other millets. Millets were boiled into a thick gravy. We also had yams and colocasia planted in our compounds. When starvation loomed, we would uproot the yam or colocasia, boil them and eat the tubers. There were other edible tubers to be found in the forest, and with no restrictions on entering the forest, meat was plentiful—we went hunting. During the night we would take a handmade torch and go into the forest. The wild hens, for instance, were easy to catch, as they did not go very high on the trees. When we got meat from hunting, we used to share it among the community.

---

[3] From mid-September to mid-October

We used to go fishing also; all these were a part of our livelihood.

Although many households in our community were starving, ours wasn't affected much, thanks to maaman's smartness. He had a special job in those days, *murichoma* cultivation. In the tribal language we used to call it *murichi*, which referred to cultivation on the landlords' lands.

Under this arrangement, the landlord would give workers under him five acres of land. He would also supply the worker with seeds and manure and lend him his buffaloes for ploughing. However, the worker would not get paid for this work and had to depend upon the paddy the landlord gave him after the harvest. So, we worked hard to get a good harvest. When it was time for harvest, we would collect it and put it in the quadrangle in the landlord's house. We would thresh the paddy there with the help of the buffaloes and later the grains would be measured.

For one acre of land, the landlord should get one pack of grain. One pack was equal to four *paras*. So, for five acres of land, the landlord would get five packs which was equal to twenty *paras* of paddy. The hay also belonged to the landlord. We had to tie everything and keep it ready for the landlord. Once the worker had given everything to the landlord, he could take whatever remained. That was how it was done. Most of the time, the labourers who worked in the five acres would get nothing. The harvest would be just enough for the landlord's share.

Maaman never worked on the entire five acres allotted to him. He would take only two acres and sublease the remaining three acres to someone else. He would then work day and night. In his two acres, he was able to get a good harvest. When the harvesting was done, even if he gave eight *paras* of paddy to the landlord, there would be more remaining. He would bring the remaining paddy and store it in a *komma*.⁴ It would then be buried, to preserve it. Thus, we never had any shortage of food. By the time I was back from school, there would be something cooked for me. But as I was full (because of all the tapioca eaten at school), I would not want anything to eat. But this plenitude did not spill over into availability of clothes.

I had a pair of khaki trousers and a shirt made of *kora* cloth, to wear to school. There were no school uniforms then. As soon as I reached home, I would take off my shirt and trousers. I would wash them once every two days. And whether they were dry or damp, the next day I had to wear the same clothes. With just one pair of trousers and a shirt, I had to manage the entire year. We bought clothes only at a particular time of the year—between the two festival seasons in Valliyoorkkavu.⁵ We had to buy clothes for the whole year on that day.

The womenfolk wore saris. We call it *chinda*. These saris did not have prints or floral designs like those we see today. The entire piece would be one solid color—black, red, blue, etc. The women would drape the sari and use it also as a blanket at night. Everything was done with one single piece. Those days there was no 'sari-blouse'. They tied the saree in one knot. The clothes were brought from Mysore. At the time of the festival, the traders would bring them to Valliyoorkkavu. We could buy from there.

---

⁴ A basket for storing grains
⁵ Valliyoorkkavu Bhagavathi temple is an ancient temple, dating back to the fourteenth century, located near Mananthavady in Wayanad. For the Adivasi communities in Wayanad, this is a place of prominence, their most important place of worship and the centre of their religious beliefs. The annual festival of this temple, which commences on the first day of the Malayalam month of Meenam (March) and lasts for a fortnight, is a major event. Historical evidence indicates that the temple was once infamous for practising bonded labour and for functioning as a market where Adivasis were sold as slaves.

6

Learning Becomes Serious Business

Maaman had another craze, just like what he had for movies. Whenever he happened to get some money, he would set off on a tour. He would travel alone to many places. Since grandfather and grandmother were old, he took care to stock-up all essentials before going on such trips. There would be enough to eat at home though maaman would return only after a week or so. However, since my grandparents were unable to do any chores, they found it difficult to look after me during these absences. This made them compel maaman to get married. But he was not at all interested.

Finally, my grandmother asked him to take me also on his tours. This was an ultimatum from her. Maaman was in a fix. Finally, he agreed to marry and got married to a woman named Kurumatti. The job assigned to her was to take care of me. Nothing else.

It was during this period that my grandfather became ill and died. I was in class two then. After that, my grandmother would visit amma and stay with her. She would also go to my mother's elder sister in Chiramoola. Once grandmother started staying with her daughters often, maaman got tired of Plamoola. He shifted to Kulirmavu, taking us with him. There were two Kulirmavus—North Kulirmavu and South

Kulirmavu. Amma's place was in South Kulirmavu. Maaman took us to North Kulirmavu.

Those days, houses were made of mud. The walls were made of bamboo sticks tied together. These were then plastered with mud, making it like an air-conditioned house. All houses belonged to the landlords. Even when we moved into another house, we were not supposed to modify or change the house. Even if we built a house with our own hands, its ultimate owner was the landlord. Each time we moved, we had to construct a new house for ourselves, while the one we left behind could be handed over by the landlord to another worker.

Afterwards, we worked from Kulirmavu. In those days, 'work' actually amounted to just slavery for us. We were allowed to go from one workplace to another. No ban on that. Once we had completed the one-year bond with the landlord, we were permitted to go. Similarly, we could shift from one locality to another. But everywhere the land belonged to the landlord. No one among us had one's own place to live. Whatever we planted on the land surrounding our house also belonged to the landlord. We could not even touch the produce—even if it was just a chilli plant. We needed the landlord's permission to pluck even one chilli. We had to often steal our own harvest to survive.

There was another aspect, too. We would clear the forest near our house and plant some crop or the other there. We used to sow ragi and other millets. Also, we would plant tubers like colocasia and yam. All these crops and vegetables growing in the forest area, we could take for our own use. No one would object to this, since we had cleared the forest and planted it ourselves.

Maaman's first child was a boy. He was named Beran. They stayed at home while I went to school. Even when we moved houses, school was never interrupted. In the early years of schooling, I was very lazy. A few of the other students from our community dropped out of school. But I couldn't escape school. Finally, there were just two students in my class—A. C. Narayanan and I. Even if we had wanted to, it was impossible for both of us to drop out. For me, it was maaman who stood in the way, and for Narayanan, it was his elder brother. Both kept strict tabs on us. We couldn't hide. There were two incidents in connection with it.

Those days lorries used to come to our area to transport hay. And the community boys would get into the lorry, and have a fun ride. The lorries had ropes to tie the hay and these ropes would be hanging free behind the lorry. We kids would hang on to this rope and go along with the lorry. The driver and cleaner would not be aware of this adventure. The kids would get down at the first place the lorry stopped. And from there they would find their way back and return home. This was how the rides went on. Once I saw a lorry that had stopped in Thrissilery. I felt like having a ride. But I hadn't attempted this before because I was afraid of maaman. That day I dared to swing from the ropes and had my first ride. The lorry stopped at Kaattikulam. As youngsters then, we did not even know there was a place called Kaattikulam. I saw two or three shops there. The lorry had stopped because people in the shops called out to the driver about our risky adventurous ride. The driver scolded us and we ran. We ran every which way we could. Finally, we reached a Paniya locality. By then it was dusk, and the people in that place did not allow us to go back at night. They knew that we children shouldn't be left alone. So, we spent the night there. The next day, they said, they would take us to Brother Maran. Maran was a village chief whom we knew. They also knew him. We had kanji and spent the night there. The next morning, we were taken to Maran. This man knew maaman very well. He asked me where I had gone and I described to him our entire adventure.

In the meanwhile, there was total chaos at our homes. Everyone went searching for the missing boys. They searched the forest and left no stone unturned. Finally, they came to know that we had gotten into the lorry and gone for a ride. As Maran Mooppan was escorting us back, halfway through we saw the people searching for us. Mooppan came all the way to our village and took each child to their respective homes. The showdown started after that. Maaman thrashed me left and right for going without permission and also for skipping school.

After this episode, I was no longer allowed to play with that group of children. This became a major issue for me. They would go out to graze cattle, and whenever I saw them, I longed to join—but I did not have permission. One day, I decided to go anyway. That day, skipping school, I went with those children. We went to the forest, grazed the cattle, ate the fruits in the forest and came back in the evening. I had hoped to reach home before maaman. But he was there before me. Maaman was under the impression that I had gone to school. When he saw the gang of children with me, he got really wild. That day also I got a thorough thrashing. He thrashed me so much that I became unconscious. My grandmother came and stopped maaman from beating me further. She scolded him after which he stopped. After a while, maaman himself bathed me in hot water. The next day onwards I stopped skipping school. I was really scared. At the same time, I also could understand how much maaman cared for me. So, I decided to take my studies seriously.

 Scan the QR code to listen to Kariyan Mooppan recount his school days in his own voice.

7

Childhood Memories

The school was upgraded class by class as we progressed each year. With every passing year, a new higher class was added, and the number of teachers grew as well. Most of them came from Thalassery, and they all liked us.

No one showed any discrimination. Even when the landlords tried to influence the teachers against us, our teachers wouldn't listen to them. Narayanan and I got special consideration and attention from the teachers.

Chandran Maash[1] joined our school when I was in class four. He liked me a lot because I showed interest in studies. I was one of the few among the tribal people to show interest in studies, and therefore, he had a special affinity towards me. How could I not study? If I did not study, I would get punished at school. If I complained about this at home, I would get punished again and told that it was because I had not studied that I was being punished at school. Under the circumstances, the better option was to study!

I had to study Malayalam, Maths, English, etc. We needed to study English only from class five onwards. We had to write with a pencil. By the time I had completed class two, I was able to read cinema notices for maaman. If I stumbled while reading, he would scold me, asking why I was being

---

[1] Maash: teacher

sent to school if I couldn't even read properly. When Chandran Maash got to know of my notice reading and maaman's cinema craze, he started compelling maaman to learn to read and write. He started advising maaman, 'Kariyan has lots to study. From now on, he will not get time to read your notices.' Finally, maaman yielded.

After four every evening, maaman would finish his work and go to Chandran Maash's house. Maash used to live in a rented house at Aashaankolli. His story is part of another thread in Wayanad's immigration story. People from places like Thalassery and Kannur would come to our area as school teachers. Later on, they brought their families too. Their descendants are still here. There was one Warrier's house in Varinilam. That house was rented out and five of our teachers lived there. Our people would go to the house to study. Like maaman, many others including M. B. Kaalan and M. B. Kariyan learnt to read and write. My classmate Narayanan's brother Maavundan was also on this list. They were all invited by these school teachers to come and learn how to read and write. These people were not able to write properly, but they could read well soon. Their writing was full of spelling errors. They wrote in their own language. Anyway, my uncle had learnt to read cinema notices; and therefore I was relieved from that duty!

When I was in class four, maaman, as usual, went on a trip after arranging all the essentials needed at home. Before starting the journey, he entrusted maami[2] to look after me and to send me to school properly. But once maaman left, I had no food. I went to school for two days without food. My grandmother was also not at home as she had gone to her daughter's house. She used to do minor household chores at her daughter's and stay on. This was because she did not see eye-to-eye with maami. That's why she stayed away.

---

[2] Maami: aunt

As days went by, I couldn't stand going to school hungry. It was mandatory that I went to school. When my maaman was around, maami would do everything properly. But her behaviour would change once he left for his trips. She would boil some colocasia and eat but wouldn't keep anything for me. Even at night, I had to sleep on an empty stomach. However, though I was starving, I continued going to school.

There was an elderly woman named Malla who lived next door. She saw what was happening at our house and scolded maami. She asked me not to stay in my house, but to come to her place and have kanji. She took me to her house and started sharing some of her kanji with me.

After five to ten days like this, I could not bear it anymore. I was completely tired. I used to get kanji from Malla grandmother only once a day. The rest of the time I would go somewhere and try to forget the hunger pangs.

When maaman returned, he found me lying in the veranda, looking tired and drained. He had gone to Mysore and returned via Coorg. I had not gone to school that day. I could not bring myself to get up and go. As soon as he saw me, his first reaction was anger: why hadn't I gone to school? He screamed that question at me. At that time Malla grandmother was around. When she heard maaman screaming at me, she got really angry. She was doing some work inside. She came out with a broom, called maaman and said, 'Come over here. I will show you what the problem is.' Maaman could not understand anything. Then she narrated all the difficulties and starvation I had undergone during his absence. He got really wild hearing this. He went straight into the house. He had brought some bangles and vessels for maami. He asked her to pack all these in a sari and to vacate the house.

And then maaman escorted maami to her house. Maaman's son was very young then and had just begun to walk. The little boy was also taken to maami's house.

Maaman reached maami's house and explained to her parents how cruel she had been to me.

He said, 'I took her in marriage. Now I'm bringing her back. I have given her everything she wanted. So, from now on, let her stay here. I do not want her to come back to me.'

Her parents had no idea what was happening. They were living in Puthankunnu near Plamoola, and Kulirmavu, where we were living, was quite a distance away. They were under the impression that their daughter was staying happily with her in-laws, like everyone else. Maaman described to them all that had happened during his absence.

He said, 'There is some *paandi* [ragi] at home. I will bring that too tomorrow. Let her remain here. I don't need her at my home.' And maaman came back to our house. He went straight to my grandmother and brought her to our house. After that, I was looked after by my grandmother.

I never ever used to visit my mother. I could not stand my mother, who had married a second time. I was not friendly with my stepfather either. My mother went into labour five times; four of those children died. They survived for a few months or a year at the most. I did not even go to see my siblings. My mother used to come home to see me. She would speak to me and if she had anything with her, she would give it to me. Those days, wages were paid in paddy. She would sell this paddy and bring me the money. But even when I got this money, I would not keep it for myself. I would give it to maaman. I did not have any need for money. I was looked after by my grandmother and she needed no money either.

But I did commit a theft once. Only once. All the children used to buy sweets from a shop near the school. There was only one shop. I did not have any money with me nor could

I ask anyone. I bore this for some days; and then one day I thought, all the children were buying sweets so I also should buy. I stole four *anas* from my uncle. Four *anas* was twenty-five paise.

That evening, on the way back from school, all of us bought flattened rice and jaggery. There were Warrier kids too among us. There was a small stream on the way, with clear water flowing over dark rocks. We all sat by the water and enjoyed the sweets we had bought. Our stomachs were pleasantly full.

There was some money left over even after buying all the sweets. I put it in my pocket and came home. When grandmother took my clothes for washing, she noticed the money in the pocket. She questioned me, asking where I had got the money. I did not answer her immediately. Then hesitantly I told her how I had gotten the money.

Grandmother kept the money and said, 'Don't you dare speak of this to your uncle. If you speak up, he'll kill you.'

I listened to her and did not say a word about it. That is the one and only theft I have ever committed in my life. I believe, maaman never got to know about this.

It was during school vacations that we had pelas. All children would be taken to attend. I was the only one who could not go. Maaman would not allow me to go. But he himself would go. The elders went to learn how to do the rituals and its procedures. They had one *aashaan* (master). His name was Chokran. There was not a thing under the sun that Chokran Mooppan did not know. Maaman and others went to Chokran Mooppan to learn things. They would go as assistants, and watch and learn how he conducted the rituals. Maaman and C. K. Janu's[3] father, Munikariyan, both went to learn from Mooppan. They were very close to each

---

[3] C. K. Janu, Adivasi activist and politician, is known for leading land rights movements, especially with the Adivasi Gothra Mahasabha, advocating for indigenous rights and social justice.

other. Whatever Chokran Mooppan knew, he taught them. The only thing they were not taught was about medicines. The two had no interest in that either. Leaving aside medical knowledge, they learnt everything else.

C. K. Janu used to stay here. Later on, she went to Panavalli to get land for the tribals. Till then she used to live here in Akkerekunnu where her homestead was.

8

Aashramam School, and then to S.K.M.J.

When I completed my fifth standard, I was sent to the aashramam school (Government Residential Basic Tribal School) in Mananthavady. The school was exclusively for tribal children. Chandran Maash took the initiative to send me there. He knew a teacher in the aashramam school. He was also from Thalassery. Chandran Maash told the teacher, 'I am sending a boy there. He studies well and he is not naughty. He won't find it difficult to stay there and learn.' That teacher agreed to admit me. Thus, I became a student of the aashramam school. Maaman was also interested in this. Whenever someone pointed out something that would be good for me, maaman showed his willingness a hundredfold.

But the problem lay elsewhere. I had only one pair of clothes which could not be used in the new school. There they used clothes made of khadi, and that too they had to be white in colour. Maaman bought me everything. At that time, he could afford it. He had enough paddy and ragi. Everything was bought with his money. But maaman would not spend a single paisa unnecessarily.

He bought all that I needed and took me to the new school. The school had many students from around the locality. There were children from Thirunelli, Bavali and Ondayangadi. All of them were tribals belonging to the Raavula and Paniya communities. There were none from the Kurichyas or Kurumans. In total, we were forty students. Our food was cooked in the school itself. Meat was served once a week, and fish on another day. The food was quite good. I got the kind of food that I never had at home. To get meat at home, we had to wait for a special occasion or some guest.

 Once I had a craving to eat meat and I played a trick to get my way. My grandmother used to rear a few hens and cocks at home. She would not sell them. She would neither give them away nor eat them. They would grow well only to be eaten by foxes. Grandmother did not mind that, but she was very strict that the hens were not to be killed and eaten. One day, maaman had spread paddy to dry in the sun. It was a school holiday. He told me, 'You shouldn't go to play anywhere today. Be here and guard the paddy from the hens.' Those days I had a small bow and arrow with me. I also had a catapult with which I could hurl stones. Maaman said, 'You keep the catapult and stones ready and stay right here.' And he went out.

 Soon, I was fed up shooing away the hens—they would keep coming back to peck at the paddy. I was getting angry. Grandmother also was not at home. So, in my anger, I hurled a stone at one of the birds. That one was a cock. The stone hit it directly on its head. The cock died, after a few minutes of writhing in pain. Now I was scared. I was sure maaman would beat me up. I feared that grandmother might also beat me up. I was thinking about what might happen. Maaman was the first to come back home.

 In the meantime, I had picked up the dead cock and placed it in the veranda where I sat. I told maaman what had happened. I didn't dare tell a lie. If he came to know I was lying, he would beat me up even more. So, I told him the truth. He told me not to panic. 'You sit there. Let's wait for mother to return.' Grandmother came and saw the dead cock. She asked what had happened to it. Maaman told her a fox had come and was about to catch the cock. What could Kariyan do all alone? So, he used the catapult to pelt a stone at the fox. It didn't hit the fox, but the fox soon left sensing danger. By that time it had already killed the cock. That's what happened. So, what to do with the dead cock? It was decided to make a chicken curry! Maaman would defend me on many occasions.

After joining the aashramam school, I lost touch with my friends in Kulirmavu. I had holidays only for occasions like Onam and Christmas. I could not get a weekly or monthly holiday in my school. They had classes only up to five. I was made to join this school only for one academic year. Whenever I came home, I longed to see the pela celebration or other such festivals. But however much I pleaded, maaman would not permit me.

Then grandmother used to say, 'Won't he also want to see all this? How can we leave him alone at home and go? I'm also going for pela. Let him come with me.' And once in a while, I got to go for pela, thanks to grandmother's intervention. But the permission came with strict instructions: I had to remain seated in one place throughout the ritual and could not join others who were having fun during the ceremony. Maaman kept watch over me as I sat under the shamianas, watching their singing and dancing.

Thus, I passed my fifth standard exams. Then Chandran Maash told my uncle about the school in Kalpetta where students can study from class five to ten. In fact, at the aashramam school, I was being prepared for this school. To study at Kalpetta, I had to stay far away from home and stay in a hostel. That was what I was being prepared for in the Mananthavady school. Chandran Maash went to Kalpetta S.K.M.J. school. The hostel warden there was one

Kunhikannan, from Koothuparamba. He was known to Chandran Maash. So Chandran Maash said he could get an admission there for me using this connection. He was sure that I could join that school.

When maaman came to know of this, he said, 'Let him go. After all, it is for studies. I don't have any problems with Kariyan going. I fully agree with the idea of him joining the school.'

Hence, I joined this school. I had to go from here by bus. There was only one bus going to Kalpetta, a private bus called CWMS that went all the way to Kozhikode. I had to take another bus back home. The bus to Kozhikode went via Kalpetta. At that time, A. C. Narayanan also passed class five. He also wanted to come to Kalpetta, and he joined the school. That meant we could get together again. All the other kids who were in class five with us in the aashramam school also joined. Chandran Maash and Bhaskaran Maash took the initiative to get all the students admitted there.

I will never forget those teachers. They taught me so well. Later on, when I returned from jail, a happy incident happened. There was a club here called Vaakku.[1] We constructed a stage for the school in the name of that club. It was solely on our own initiative, and for its inauguration, we invited our teachers. It was a programme held to pay tribute to our teachers. They all came for that function. And then they returned to Thalassery.

I can never forget those two teachers. There was yet another teacher, Gopalakrishnan Maash, headmaster of the Kalpetta school. I will never forget him also.

---

[1] 'Vaakku' means 'word'

9

The Memories of S.K.M.J.

I do not remember the exact years when I studied at S.K.M.J.[1] Anyways, I remember I was there in 1962. The reason to remember that year is the India–China war. During the war, all students went around collecting donations. I studied till class nine there. I lost a year in-between. Then I had to take re-admission. After that I went to jail. Those days there were no scholarships for ST children to study. Food and accommodation were free. We also got books. The other children had to pay for their food. They had to buy books. Also, we never got any help in terms of money.

Those Kalpetta times were such amazing days. The hostel, the Gandhi Sadan hostel, belonged to the management. It's not there anymore. The school belonged to M. K. Jinachandran. He had constructed this hostel too. It had children from all castes. It was meant for children coming from faraway places to stay and study. There was

---

[1] S.K.M.J.H.S.S. (Shubha Krishna Memorial Jain Higher Secondary School). S.K.M.J.H.S.S. in Kalpetta was the first high school in Wayanad district. It was established in 1944 by M. K. Jinachandran. After its inception, students from Wayanad did not have to depend on schools in other districts for high school education. The students came from various distant parts of Wayanad, and therefore, a hostel facility was established from the initial days. Currently, S.K.M.J. is a higher secondary school.

no non-vegetarian food there, only vegetarian. It was because the school belonged to the Jain community. There would be their special prayer to God. After the prayer was study time. There was no discriminations or untouchability there.

Kalpetta brought about a great change in me as a student. I was always seen as a good student. But one subject remained my stumbling block. I just about managed to pass the Hindi exams. Even when I tried to overcome this barrier, I couldn't make any progress. I would somehow scrape through. No amount of tapasya would help me out to score more than the pass minimum. I would score good marks in all the other subjects. For science and other subjects, I used to cry in front of the teacher for an extra mark. In those days science was not divided into different branches, only science. It had all the topics covered.

I liked science best out of all subjects I had to study. During one of the years in Kalpetta, I answered all the questions in the science question paper correctly. I would never take a break after the exams. I would check my notes, check if I have answered the questions correctly and calculate the marks I was about to get. Then I would keep the question paper safe. When the teacher returned the answer sheet, I had scored 98. But my calculation showed 100. I counted and recounted. It still came up 100. Also, the teacher had not marked any answer as incorrect. And I started crying. The teacher came and asked what had happened. I told her that I had answered everything correctly, but 'why did you deduct two marks'. She said it wasn't proper to give 100 out of 100. Then seeing me inconsolable, she agreed to add one mark to the total. And my total came to 99! I was such a student.

Not just my studies, Kalpetta changed me a lot as a person. It was during this time that I had this idea of changing my name. It was the time when I had passed from class six to seven. The kid who used to come to school with me was called Narayanan. My name is Kariyan. No other kid in that school had a name like mine. I felt ashamed of my name. I was really unhappy. It was maaman who had given me my name. The full name is Kariyappan. It was derived from the name of a Coorgi god.

I was unhappy because my name revealed my community. I asked many people if it was possible to change my name. I even asked my teachers. One teacher told me, 'See, it's not easy to change one's given name. You need to get published in the gazette to change your name. This is not a child's play.' Then I went directly to the headmaster, Gopalakrishnan Maash. He knew the details of all the students in the school. He used to give special tuition to the backward students in every class. He wanted to make sure that no one failed.

I went to see the headmaster with the hope that he would help me. Gopalakrishnan Maash was from somewhere in Kozhikode. He was an able teacher and commanded a lot of respect and fear. Just the sight of him was enough to make the students keep quiet. Everyone respected him so much.

So, I went to him and told him, 'Sir, I want to change my name.'

He asked me, 'What's wrong with your name?'

I said that it didn't sound good when people called me by that name, and that I was the only one in the entire school with this name. 'I want to change my name.'

He said, 'A name is given to identify a person. It's not some kind of a label to stick on your forehead. So, better keep your name. You don't need to find a new name now. That's not going to work. I will not allow that either. Go back to class.'

I was so disappointed and unhappy as I went back. Our English teacher, Seshadri Iyer, was taking the class. Everyone was scared of him. If we made even the smallest mistake, he would shout, 'Did you come to class after eating shit this morning?'

When I entered the class, my face showed all my disappointment. He asked me, 'Why so glum?'.

There was this friend who used to sit with me in class, one Venugopal. He replied, 'Sir, he had gone to get his name changed. But the headmaster wouldn't allow it. He's sad because of that.'

Then the teacher said, 'What's wrong with your name? There is not much in a name. Just look at my name. I am called Seshadri Iyer. What is so special about that name? Do you know anyone else with that name? Be proud that you are the only one with your name. So, it will do for you. We both can keep our names.'

That was the end of my desire to change my name.

 Scan the QR code to hear this episode in Kariyan Mooppan's own voice.

10

An Unforgettable Episode

―••●••―

As life continued in this manner, I happened to come home for vacation. By then maaman had relocated to Kaithavally. He had also married again; his wife's name was Chikki. She was from Plamoola, a good woman who would take care of everything. She had a son, Kolumban. That was my grandfather's name. It was my grandmother who named him after my grandfather.

When I was studying in Kalpetta, whenever I wrote to him asking for something, maaman would come to Kalpetta and see me. He would buy me whatever I wanted and then return. Since the teachers had taught him to read, maaman was able to read my letters. But he had difficulty writing.

And so the days passed. After maaman's second marriage, he got entangled in a love affair. Her name was Poochathi. Maaman was in Kaithavally with her till he died. He thought that he could look after two wives at the same time. But the community did not permit that. As per our community rules, a man should have only one wife. Poochathi too remained unmarried till death. Maaman took care of everything in her house. She died only after he had passed away. Till his death, he used to take care of both the households. Since maaman was the Mooppan of the community, nobody questioned him. Who would dare?

During the vacation, I first went to Plamoola. When I reached, I found that maami wouldn't speak to me. She was angry as well as sad that maaman had begun a new relationship. I wasn't aware of what was going on. Later on, I came to know of all that had happened from other people. Maaman was still in Kaithavally. And so, I went to Kaithavally. Maaman was there. And I found a few kids to play with. I became quite friendly with them. For a few years, this friendship continued.

All of them used to go to a nearby tea shop to have tea. For these children, the trip to the tea shop was one great event. I too felt like going to the tea shop. Maaman told me to go and have tea with them. Gave me money also. Thus, I too went to the tea shop. I had an unforgettable experience there. One terrible experience. Especially because I had never ever had such an experience earlier in my life. I came to know how deep and painful the wound of being insulted is. This was a learning experience which changed my outlook.

We used to call that shop 'school shop'. That shop was run by one Andruman, from Thalassery. I can never forget his name. That is yet another secret. Anyway, I went to the shop and placed an order for tea. He brought me tea. I was alone. He asked me about my school. He wanted to know whether there were many shops near my school. I was explaining things to him while having the hot tea and an unda.[1] Then a Warrier came into the shop. Andruman had given me tea in a glass tumbler commonly given to all. He did not discriminate between people. His principle was if you want tea, you can have it in the same tumbler, or else you can just leave it and go. That was how he was. He used to justify this saying, 'Everyone pays me money for having tea. The tribals pay their hard-earned money, while the upper-caste people never have to toil for their money. Money earned through hard toil is much more valuable. This is my

---

[1] Unda is a sweet snack shaped into small round balls.

livelihood. So, if the tribals give me money, I will give them their money's worth. I can't bring in a new tumbler just for you. I don't have it.'

Those days, some people would serve tribals tea in coconut shells. This Andruman was not one among them. He was a gem of a man. When the Warrier reached the tea shop, I was sipping my tea. His name was Kunhiraman. As soon as he saw me sitting on the bench, he shouted, 'Get up, you brat.' Andruman was inside the shop doing something. When he heard the Warrier's loud voice, he came out. I was frightened. I was in class seven or so at that time. I staggered up in fear.

Then Andruman came to me, held me by my shoulders and asked me to sit down and finish my tea.

The Warrier then tried to scare Andruman. 'What! When higher class people like us come to your shop, you would allow a tribal to sit on the bench and have tea? Ask him to take his tea and go elsewhere to drink it,' he said.

Andruman replied, 'This is my place. My shop. I am the one who decides who should come here and who should not. This boy came to have tea. He won't steal anything from here when he leaves after finishing his tea. This bench on which he is sitting will be here. So also, the shop. If you have come to buy something, you can have it. And you can sit here. There are other benches here. You don't have to make him get up from the bench he is sitting on. Do understand that you won't sit here after making the boy get up.'

The Warrier got really angry and he stomped out of the shop, saying, 'I don't want any of your stuff.'

Andruman called out to him, 'People like you pay me only once a year. [They used to have an account in the tea shop and they paid the whole amount once a year only at the time of harvest.] Unlike you, these tribals pay me daily from what they get as daily wages. It's from their money that I cater to all your needs.'

Hearing all this, I was quite upset. I did not feel like having the tea. I wanted nothing. I just wanted to go home.

Seeing my state, Andruman told me, 'Don't be scared, son. No idea which century these guys still live in. If this had happened in my place, this man would not have his head above his shoulders. You study well and get into a good position. Then the same man would bend before you with folded hands. That's how your revenge should be.' He gave me a sweet before sending me home.

Those days Varghese[2] used to come to this place. He and his comrades had organised a strike because the workers were not being given their wages. The landlords were seething with anger because of all these incidents. The showdown at the tea shop was an expression of their general anger. All the landlords joined together and decided to attack the striking workers by bringing in professional goondas. In those days there were only Adivasis in the area. The Kurichyas, Kurumas, Paniyars, Raavulas, etc., were supporting Varghese. We were also joined by a few immigrant workers who also worked for daily wages. What could they do when they were not given their wages? So they also had their problems with the landlords.

Things were beginning to change. People started working towards freedom from bonded labour and a better life, rather than waiting passively for things to change. As a result of this, our people started seeking work from the immigrants too. If we worked for them, we would be given tapioca or something else to eat in the evening when the

---

[2] Arikkad Varghese, popularly known as 'Naxal Varghese', was a revolutionary leader from Kerala active in the late 1960s. Associated with the Naxalite movement, he championed tribal rights in Wayanad. He worked among the Adivasi communities and highlighted their exploitation by landlords and forest contractors. He was arrested in 1970, and was shot dead while in police custody. Decades later, a police constable, P. Ramachandran Nair, confessed that it was a staged encounter killing carried out under orders from higher authorities. Varghese has become a symbol of revolutionary political activism in Kerala.

work was done. We also got our wages. This meant we had some money when we got home. They never gave us paddy because it wasn't part of their cultivation. They had money that they got from selling each day's produce. They gave wages out of this money. Thus, it was much better to work for the immigrants than going to the landlords. Thus the landlords were angry with us for going to work for the immigrants.

At Valliyoorkkavu, the landlords renewed our bonds of service. At that time, we also had to repay whatever money we had borrowed from them during the year. Some of us were able to repay the full amount. Some could not. Those who could not completely repay the amount would have the outstanding added to the next year's payment. So, they had to continue the bonded labour for another year. They could never free themselves from it. Till the time the immigrants came, even those who had completely repaid their amount, had to work under the landlords. Once the immigrants came, we started getting daily wages from them and it was a huge relief for us. From then on, those of us who could fully repay the landlords chose not to work for them any longer. If we kept a bond with a landlord, we could only work for that landlord. If there is no bond, we could go to anyone who called us to work. Seeing this, others who still owed money to the landlords managed to repay the full amount and freed themselves from bonded labour.

That was how the strike for wages began. I don't have any first-hand experience of the beginning of this strike. I was not here but at school in Kalpetta. I recall Varghese coming to us, even when I was studying here. But I never would see him often and did not get to know him. Maaman would not let me go out. If I had gone out and mingled with other people, I would have known all that was happening around me. Varghese used to come when I was in Thrissilery as well as when I was in Mananthavady. But I knew nothing about what was happening.

11
The Gods Continue Their Journey

―••●••―

When the gods started the journey, passing through forests and hills on the way, they were going north. Their mothers Aaryanaka and Baaniyagunba gave them directions. The mothers told the gods that they would be able to find a solution for their problems, if they travelled north. Thus, the gods, who went on and on towards north, finally reached a marshy land and saw a strange sight: a strange being submerged in the marsh, with just its hands and head above the slush, was gathering and eating the mud and fungus around it. At first glance, it looked like a female figure.

As the gods were crossing over this area and going forward, the being asked, 'Where are you all rushing off to? It seems you don't even have a moment to speak to one another.'

'We are on a long journey. Who are you?' the gods asked a question in reply.

The being said, 'I am Kinaanthi, the goddess—ever-present, all-pervading throughout the universe.' Then again Kinaanthi asked, 'Why are you in a hurry?'

The gods said, 'We created humans, and gave them life too. But they cannot talk or get up and walk.' The gods shared their sorrow.

Kinaanthi promised to help them. She said she could make humans talk and walk. But there was a condition. 'When the human starts talking and walking, whoever is within my reach, I will eat them up,' said Kinaanthi. Hearing this condition, the gods were a little worried. Then they discussed this offer among themselves and finally accepted it.

'In that case, I need Aariyapaitha's upper cloth, and also Baaniyapaitha's upper cloth,' Kinaanthi said.

The gods gave her the upper cloth. Then she said, 'I am naked and I wish to drape this upper cloth upon myself. For this, you gods must turn your backs toward me, each of you holding an open straw umbrella in your hands.'

The gods agreed and did just that. Kinaanthi draped Aariypaitha's upper cloth around her waist and with Baaniyapaitha's upper cloth she covered her breast. She asked the gods to return to their palace and that she would come there after taking a shower. The gods agreed to that too. They went back to their palace.

After some time, Kinaanthi descended upon the human forms fashioned by the gods—her thousand hands outstretched, her tongue reaching down to her bosom, teeth jagged and sharp, eyes rolling like globes, her voice a thunderous roar. Swift as a storm, her vast and terrible form rose to touch the very sky. The terrified forms got up and started running around, crying out pleadingly. From among these humans, the ones who shouted 'Aarada' evolved into Brahmins. The ones who made the sound 'ep' became the Raavulas, and the ones who shouted 'apay' became the Paniyas. This is the story of our origin.

But one can see a variation of the story in Raavula's Pulapattu. This other story goes like this:

That terrifying monster, after giving humans the ability to talk and walk, just like she had told the gods, started eating up the humans one by one. Finally, there were only two humans left. They kept on running to save themselves. First they reached Thirunelli and then Thrissilery. Then they reached a place called Paakkam. They saw a fort there and ran into it. They hid themselves in the plantain plantation there. This was noticed by Paakkathappan who inhabited the fortress. He also saw the terrifying figure catching up with the humans. When that figure reached the door of the fortress, the door became too small for the huge figure to enter. Paakkathappan came near the door and asked her, 'Who are you? What do you want?'

That figure replied, 'I'm Maali. Two humans who were supposed to be my food have taken asylum in this fort. I want them.'

'Okay, I can give them to you. They are here. Let me have my shower and food, then I will come and meet you. Till then, you take rest under that jackfruit tree,' Paakkathappan said. Maali agreed. She sat under the jackfruit tree, waiting. The two human beings, now under the hope that they were safe from the huge figure, also waited inside the fortress.

And they continued to wait.

12

That One Year I Skipped School

It was after class eight that I skipped school for one full year. The reason was a fabric called terilyn! Now when I think of that, I feel like laughing. That was a period when everyone got shirts stitched out of terilyn. I also wanted a similar shirt. All my fellow students had these shirts and they used to flaunt them. Those days students in S.K.M.J. had to wear a uniform—blue and white. Even now the uniform is the same. I was fed up wearing the same uniform again and again; and hence this fascination for a terilyn shirt. I wrote to maaman asking for one. I got a reply saying he did not have enough money right then but would buy one as soon as he got the money and bring it to me. I waited for a week. Maaman did not show up. I did not get my shirt either. By then, I was very keen on getting a terilyn shirt. I took permission from the hostel saying I had to go home and would come back soon. But I got back to school only after a year.

When I reached Kaithavally, maaman was not there. He was in Bairakuppa. Those days, maaman had a new job. He used to procure bamboo for Mavoor Gwalior Rayons factory. The bamboo was collected from the forest in Wayanad and transported through agents. Maaman was one such agent. He used to procure bamboo from places like Bairakuppa near Bavali, Chekuthankooppu and Antarsanta. He had built a shed there and took a few people from here to help him in cutting bamboo and for other work. When I came to know that maaman was there, I went to that place.

I met maaman and told him that I want a terilyn shirt. I just about escaped a thrashing from him. He said, 'Didn't I tell you that I would bring it to you?' He said he hadn't yet got the money for the bamboo already delivered. He couldn't even pay wages to the workers. It was in this dire situation that I had gone asking for a shirt. But I was adamant. I told him to either buy me the fabric for the shirt or give me money to buy it. 'I will return to school only after that,' I insisted. Maaman said, 'Anyway you have come all the way. So stay back here.'

He was expecting money that week after transporting the bamboo. The money had to come from Kozhikode. He had to go to the branch office in Kaattikulam and collect money from there. Since I was there, maaman decided to go home for a few days. He asked me to write down the accounts when he was away. He gave me all necessary instructions to take care of everything in his absence. Apart from keeping the accounts, I had to report how many bamboos were cut each day. And then write the number against each worker's name. I had to be very accurate. Some workers had the tendency to cheat. They would keep one small bamboo shoot in the bundle and try to pass it as a big bamboo stem. I had to be very careful about all these. This was the job given to me. He also arranged two of the workers as my assistants and even gave them money for tea and other necessities.

Thus, I remained there for a few days helping maaman. We worked in a forest area where bamboo grew, and we stayed in Bairakuppa. In Bairakuppa, there was a small shop from where we got our food in the morning. A lorry would come to the forest to load bamboo. The workers were taken in that lorry. Otherwise, if they chose to walk, they would arrive at the spot only by afternoon—it was so far away. Moreover, they had to cross an area inhabited by elephants. In the evening, after work, the workers would walk back. In the bamboo cutting area there would always be a standby of two loads of bamboo in stock. It was stocked there so that the lorry could take it back when the workers were brought back.

To take loads of bamboo out of the forest, one had to have a pass written by the agent (the one in charge of cutting the bamboo). There was a local Muslim man there. Since maaman could not write properly, he used to take help from this Muslim man to get the passes written. And then it would be sent along with the lorries in the morning. The passes had to have all the details like the number of the lorry, how many bamboos were loaded, the driver's name, etc. Otherwise, they would be confiscated by forest guards as unauthorised exports. The forest area was partly in Karnataka and partly in Kerala. So there was more trouble. Maaman had told me all these details before leaving for home. He also showed me samples of written passes. In addition, the Muslim man who used to write them, gave me further details. He told me, 'You know how to read and write. So you can write the passes now and just scroll a signature of your uncle at the bottom of it.' I started writing the passes.

After a week, we got the money—two weeks' money came in one lot. The lorry driver came to me and said, 'The money's come. But you need to go to Kaattikulam and get it.'

The only way to get information was when the lorry came to load bamboo. There was no other means of communication. I sent someone to maaman, to Kaithavally. Maaman by then was involved in the strike. The one who went to get him was also from Kaithavally. So, he stayed back home for a day. The next day, both of them went to

Kaattikulam and got the money. We were in the forest at that time.

There was a bus from Mananthavady to Bavali in those days, called Shri Rama Motors. It started its trip from Thalassery. So we had to get down at Bavali and walk to Bairakuppa. And from there to the bamboo cutting area. After work, some of us would return on foot. I never did. I would get on the lorry. Because I was scared of elephants. Once I had tried walking; and that day, I was chased by an elephant. My fear of elephants increased after this. Actually, it was the fallout of a prank played by the workers. One day, it was time to return after bamboo cutting. As I counted the bamboo and wrote the accounts, I saw an elephant calf. There were two workers called Chokran and Mallan working there. As soon as they saw the elephant calf, they went after it to catch it. The mother elephant was not seen anywhere near. But when the two went to tie up the calf, the mother elephant came trumpeting in anger, followed by a male elephant. All of us started running in all directions. I climbed a coral tree to save myself. In my fear, I didn't even notice it was a thorny coral tree. I had to sit there all night, and got down only after I was assured that the elephants had returned to deep forest. After that incident I never accompanied the workers who walked.

Maaman returned after getting the money. We finished the work early that day and went back from the bamboo cutting area. When I reached Bairakuppa, maaman was sitting in the shop there. I had come early and the others were yet to reach; I had gotten on the lorry to return. Not everybody could climb the bamboo bundles in the truck. Maaman then asked me to calculate everyone's account. I did, and we found that each worker had a considerable amount due. In those days, it was a really big sum. Maaman distributed the money and cleared the accounts in the shop. Even after that there was some money left. Maaman gave me some money out of it and asked me to buy a terilyn shirt and go back to school. It had been several days since I left school, so maaman wanted me to go back as soon as possible. I had come for the shirt. Now that I had the money, I was supposed to go back to school.

I agreed to go to school, took the money, but promptly went in another direction, to Antarsanta, by lorry. And from there, I went to Mysore. For two days I roamed around these places and then returned to Bairakuppa. Those days, there was a direct bus from Mysore to Bairakuppa. I reached there, hoping maaman wouldn't notice me. He would be in Bairakuppa supervising the bamboo cutting. If he spotted me it would be problematic. For him, I was supposed to be in school. Hiding from him, I left for Mananthavady. I bought the material for a shirt. From there, I went to my amma's sister's house. I stayed there for two days and again came back to Bairakuppa. This time, maaman saw me and asked me why I was not back in school. I lied that my name had been struck off from the school register.

Maaman never got to know the truth. Since I had stayed away from school for two weeks I had become lazy and did not want to go back. My desire to study had somehow disappeared. That was because I had earned some money. I now felt that if I stayed here, I could earn even more. After all, even if I studied and found a job, it would only be for money. Since I could already earn money this way, I thought there was no need to study. But maaman was not happy with it. He kept on asking what could be done to continue my studies. I came out with another lie. I said I had asked my teacher in school, he had advised me to take re-admission the next year. That year my name had already been struck off from the register. Therefore, it was not possible to go to school now. In fact, I hadn't even gone anywhere near Kalpetta. When I realised I could earn money here, it felt like heaven to me. Thus, poor maaman believed all the lies I told to him.

Since I was not going to school anyway, maaman thought I could stay back there and work with him. I also had the same wish. I knew that maaman wanted me to write the accounts. It was then that he asked me to join the workers in cutting bamboo, saying that since I was staying back I had to help and cut bamboo as well as write accounts. I did not think much of it and joined the workers to cut bamboo. Only when I reached the forest did I understand how difficult the work was. How would I know how to cut among the thorns of the bamboo stem? The workers would take a stick and beat the stalk four times and the stalk would break. But even sixteen strikes from me wouldn't do the job. It took me a whole day to cut a bamboo stalk, and that too after much difficulty. By then my palms were cut and bleeding. Thorns pricked in and I was drained. That day I stopped cutting and just wrote the accounts. When maaman came to supervise the work, he asked how many bamboos I could cut. An elderly worker named Chathan answered for me: 'Him? He could manage just one bamboo—that's lying there. If you send him again, we'll all have to stop work to bury him. So don't ask him to cut bamboo.' When maaman saw my hands bleeding, he was also sad. Maaman then gave me the complete charge of overseeing the bamboo cutting and went to Kaithavally—just what I wanted. He would come once a week. If we wanted to get the money for the bamboo deliveries, he had to come and get it. He would give me money for my expenses and take the rest with him. In those days, maaman had to take care of two households. When he went home, I was the unquestioned king there!

Once we got into trouble. There was one Maaraar[1] who used to cut bamboo around the same area—Govindan

---

[1] The Maaraar caste in Kerala belongs to the Ambalavasi community, traditionally associated with performing chores in temples. They served as temple drummers and performers of ritual music, especially with instruments like chenda and ilathalam.

Maaraar. Most of his workers were men from Kaithavally, and a few Gounders from Bairakuppa. Once we started working there, these two groups of people came to us for work. No one liked working for Maaraar because he wouldn't give proper wages. With these people coming to us, there were almost seventy to seventy-five workers with us. With so many workers cutting bamboo, multiple loads were taken out daily. The workers themselves would drag the cut bamboo and keep them in lots. I was the one in charge of counting these. Whenever I went to the forest, I would count the previous day's harvest, and the day's harvest would be counted the next day, since if I waited till the workers finished cutting, I would not be in time to catch the lorry back and would have to walk back with the workers. When Maaraar saw the amount of bamboo we could collect and how busy we were, he couldn't bear it. He paid some people to set fire to our loads of bamboo. We used to spread the load on the ground in a wide clearing. The place was called Chekuthankooppu. One had to travel further from Mettikuppa to reach there. The next day when we arrived, we could see our load on fire. We were really sad. The workers somehow put out the fire with water. And later when we sorted out the surviving good pieces of bamboo, we could only get two loads of bamboo. We informed maaman about this. He reached there immediately. He was so upset. He said, 'Let's stop this. If this goes on like this, they will not hesitate to finish off our people. Let's just leave.' Thus, we had to stop the bamboo business. After that I stayed at home; I had no other work.

13

Thrissilery and Varghese

After coming back from Bairakuppa, I did go to work in a few places here. But there was no regular work. Maaman could not look after everything on his own. So, I began working to help him. It was during this period that I got acquainted with Varghese. But he had been around for some time already. Earlier, he was a communist; but later on, he turned to Naxalism.

If I remember correctly, he had been here three years before the Thalassery–Pulpally attack. It was during this period that the strike for better wages took place here. After this strike the practice of giving one and a half ser[1] of paddy as wages stopped. Once they started getting proper wages, people began trusting Varghese. Out of this love and trust, they hid Varghese from the police for two years, without anyone's knowledge. He threatened all the landlords. I have already narrated my experience in the tea shop. During this strike period, yet another such incident happened here. I really love that incident.

A boy from our tribe was beaten up by a Warrier. This boy was in charge of looking after his cattle. He was careless and the cattle ate the paddy seedlings on the field. That was why

---

[1] 1 ser ≈ 0.933 kilogram (in British Indian standards, it was about 933 grams). In local usage, people often rounded it as roughly one kilogram.

he was thrashed. Varghese came to know of this. He came, took this boy and a few others with him, and went to see the Warrier. He was told that they had something to tell him, which brought him out of his house. When he was in the front yard of his house, Varghese lifted the small boy and asked him to slap the Warrier. The Warrier was much taller than the boy, but the boy didn't hesitate—he gave him two tight slaps across the face. Another boy who was with him also jumped up and slapped the Warrier. Everyone was happy about this incident. When I came to know about this and of why the Warrier got slapped, I couldn't control my happiness. He deserved that—not just two slaps but more. I started thinking of all those like the Warrier, who deserved a few slaps.

When I was studying in Kalpetta, I did not face any caste discrimination. The children studying there did not care about differences in caste or religion or about untouchability. Nor was there any such discrimination in the hostel or school. Everyone was the same there. That was the school rule. There was no caste hierarchy. All the children had come there to study. That was Jinachandran's order. Whenever there was a holiday there, my friends used to say, 'Why are you staying back in the hostel?' And they would ask me to go along to their houses; and I used to go. They never considered me a Raavula during these visits. Nor was I conscious about it. Everything was good. After seeing all that, I used to wonder why was it so different in my place. There were interior villages with Nairs and Nambiars[2] where there were such discriminations. I never had such experiences. I experienced it only when I came back to my place. I used to feel that my place was such a problematic place. And so, I was so happy about the strike, and especially when the high-caste Warrier was beaten up.

---

[2] Nambiars are a sub-group of the Nair community in Kerala, traditionally landholding gentry, known for martial heritage and social influence.

I felt change was coming to my place also. But I was not allowed to be part of any of these strikes.

Maaman was an active participant in the strikes. He was one of the leaders. There used to be farmers unions associated with the Marxist party. Varghese first came to our place as a leader of this union. Those days everyone here was a follower of the Marxist party. Everyone was under Varghese's leadership. He taught us to stand up for ourselves whenever someone treated us as inferior. The landlords got scared. Now they wouldn't dare to say much to our people. Before all this, when we went to work in the morning, they used to abuse us in a vulgar manner, saying things like, 'What! Are you sleeping off, after eating shit in the morning?'

All these changed with the coming of Varghese. They started to speak to us in a respectful tone, asking us to come and work. Both men and women were part of the strike. When the landlords refused to agree to our demands, we stopped the harvesting work. Then a few Warriers got down to harvesting the paddy, challenging us. They said, 'These are our fields, so we will harvest the crops ourselves.' And the striking people said, 'Okay. Go ahead and start harvesting yourselves. But don't hire any outside workers.'

What could the Warriers do? None of them, men nor women, knew how to harvest. When they tried doing the work, they cut their hands and it was all messy. Then they went home realising that the job was not meant for them. Harvesting required bending constantly, and soon they began to have backaches. Eventually, they said, 'We cannot do this job,' and left. This was how our last strike succeeded. The landlords agreed to all our demands, every one of the demands. Varghese was the sole leader of this movement.

Varghese led the initial activities. Our community trusted Varghese fully, because of the way Varghese went about doing things. He was quite different from the other leaders we had seen. There were leaders who would come and talk to us, and once they got hungry, they would go to the landlord's house. They had their food from the landlord's place. They say many prominent communist leaders had come here before Varghese's arrival. I don't know much about it. Leaders like EMS and AKG[3] had stayed in our place, undercover. Even these leaders were not very close to us.

Varghese was completely different from all these leaders we had known. He would talk to us a lot. We used to call kanji 'nuka'. Whenever hungry, he would say, 'Give me some nuka, fast.' He felt so free with us. Whatever we cooked in our houses, he would sit with us and have it without any hesitation. And he used to walk along with us. That itself was a big thing for us. Those who had come earlier would not even take a glass of water from us. And this guy was mingling with us so freely. So, all of us had great respect for him.

You want to know how my people addressed Varghese? It was a highly respectable name—Peruman—a title given to someone of high status. We used to call the elders among us by that name. We gave that name to Varghese. And he deserved that. He was a young man, and as per custom, he was not old enough to be called Peruman. He used to be very friendly with all of us.

First of all, he knew everyone in the Thirunelli–Thrissilery area. At night, if a house had only women, they would gladly unroll a mat in the veranda for him to sleep. When the men returned and saw someone outside, they would call, 'Who's there?' If the reply was, 'It's Peruman,' they would not say a word. Everyone, men or women, had utmost trust in him. When I saw all this I started to believe that Varghese was the true leader. All the others would tell us sugar-coated words and cheat us behind our backs. With each passing day and incident, my respect for Varghese grew stronger. I had this strong wish to meet the comrade in person.

---

[3] E. M. S. Namboodiripad and A. K. Gopalan, prominent early leaders of the Indian communist movement

14

Meeting Varghese

Those days the farm labourers' union meeting would be conducted in each member's home, by turns. Maaman was the secretary of the committee here. There was a Kurichya called Dhairu. He was the president. Only these two among us could speak with confidence and courage. That was why everyone decided on selecting them for these posts.

Varghese was not an office bearer in the union. But he used to be around to conduct meetings. Though he was not in a leadership position, he would be there to put into action whatever the committee resolved. But he wouldn't try to guide us or tell us what to do. In the initial stages, he used to explain the outcomes and consequences of every decision taken. But later on, he stepped aside, giving us complete autonomy. He would be there to support whatever decision was taken by the committee. Everything went on smoothly. Though I had heard much about Varghese, I hadn't seen him in person. I wanted to meet him badly.

Once, a meeting was to be held in maaman's house at Kaithavally. Those days, people used to come for the meeting from Thrissilery and other places. When they came to the meeting each one would bring something, like tea dust, sugar, or similar items. They would not turn up empty handed saying it's just a meeting. They didn't want to be a burden on the person in whose house the meeting was being conducted. Whatever each person could bring they would. These meetings would be conducted whenever an urgent matter popped up. That day, I went to maaman's house, where the meeting was to be held. I was sitting in the veranda and the first person to reach was Varghese himself. Maaman was not there at that time. Maami, her son, and I were there. I was playing with the little boy, keeping him entertained. Varghese entered, though I didn't know it was him at the time—I had never seen him before. As soon as he walked in, he asked, 'Isn't Kaalan at home?' When maami heard this from inside, she came out running. She knew Varghese. She unrolled a mat and invited him to sit. She said 'athiyule', which in our language meant 'come and sit'. Varghese knew our language very well. He had learnt it and he could speak it too.

Seeing this warm welcome from maami, I asked her who he was. She told me, 'It's Varghese Peruman.' That was my first encounter with him. The picture I had in mind was one of an old man, since he was called a Peruman by all these people. But this was one young man standing before me. He was very good looking. He had a thick moustache. If my memory is correct, he was wearing a red shirt that day. I haven't seen him in white shirt much. He was always walking on these dusty roads and some dust would stay on the shirt. Whenever he felt like lying down, he just sprawled himself wherever. He didn't want any mat or pillow. He would cover himself with his mundu. But there was a dress code for meetings. He was a volunteer captain at the time. That was my first meeting with Varghese.

He already knew me. Though he hadn't met me, he knew me from conversations with maaman. He knew that I was studying in Kalpetta and he asked me, 'Aren't you Kariyan?' I said yes to that.

'Do you know who I am?'

I replied that maami had just told me who he was.

'Had you heard about me prior to that?' he asked.

I said, 'Yes. But in my mind, you were not a young man like this. I had imagined you to be an old person.'

He said, 'Do you think old people can walk around climbing all these hills and mountains? Only youngsters like us can. So let's give the elders some rest—let the youngsters do the walking.'

He asked me which class I was in. Then I told him the lie I had been telling everyone—that my name had been struck off from the school register.

'Hey fellow, I know everything. You are cheating your maaman. And that's how you are here. Does any school strike a student's name off for being absent for one week?'

Till then no one had asked such a question because no one in my community knew much about all this. He was the first one to ask.

And he said, 'If a school has to strike off a name, there should be fifteen days of unauthorised absence. Even then, certain formalities are followed. First, they send a letter to your home and wait for a reply. Only if there's no response will they strike off your name. Who are you trying to fool?'

And I became aware of the fact that there were some rules, and to strike off my name, there were formalities like that.

Then he advised me a lot. He told me, 'From tomorrow onwards you have to go to school. You have to study well. Haven't you seen these people on strike? Once youngsters like you study well and reach high positions, your people will not have to go on strikes. You'll be able to speak up for them and secure all concessions yourself. Your people won't have to bow to anyone to get things done—you can do it for them.'

He talked a lot in this vein and advised and motivated me to study. By that time maami had made tea. And people started arriving one by one for the meeting. I went inside and sat there. Once all of them dispersed after the meeting, I felt I had to see Varghese once more. I had a lot to talk to him about.

From then on, whenever I got an inkling that Varghese was coming to a place, I would make sure to be there. I would join as a part of the group there. Then Varghese would explain politics in detail. In those days, Varghese was still a communist. It was some time later that he had differences with the party. He was here during that period as well. He would visit his house in Vellamunda only on rare occasions. Even then, he wouldn't stay at home. If you wanted to meet him, you had to go to Thrissilery or Thirunelli. His base was our locality, where he had people who could understand him and who were ready to obey him. That was why he stayed back here till the very end.

The party had assigned workers to different areas to spread its base. That was how Varghese had first come here. He was the party secretary at Kannur. He came here from there. Earlier also people had been sent like this. But the landlords here had good influence with the party; so whoever was sent by the party had joined the landlords. How could they then help grow the party? When the party noticed that nothing good was happening here, they sent Varghese. It was only after Varghese arrived here that the party grew significantly. Otherwise, nothing would have happened for the party in this place.

Whenever Varghese saw me, he would advise me to go to school the next year. 'It won't do any good to you, loitering around here like this. I don't like it at all.'

If I hadn't met Varghese then and if Varghese hadn't told me to go back to school, I wouldn't have ever gone back to school. I would have devised another lie to stay out of school. In fact, my decision was to not go to school at all. Anyway, I got enough money working here.

Varghese guessed that and told me that the daily wages I got was nothing. 'It will last only for the day. Nothing more will come of it. Even if you work hard until evening, what will you really gain here? You're still a child—they won't pay you the full wages given to a grown man,' he said.

Hearing all this my mind changed. His words did get me to go back to school. Otherwise, I wouldn't have gone back to school at all.

 Scan the QR code to hear Kariyan Mooppan recall his first encounter with Varghese, in his own voice.

15

Memories of Varghese

Meanwhile, I had also made an attempt to run off to Pulpally without anyone's knowledge. A lot of people were migrating to this area, to the lands belonging to the Devaswam.[1] There were a lot of encroachments taking place in areas like Sasimala. And I went too. It was Varghese who found me and brought me back here.

Pulpally was the centre of a lot of immigration. Those who came encroached into the forest land there. Sasimala was a dense forest then. When I came to know all this, I too thought why not go there and encroach into some forest land and make it my own? Amma's sister was in Chirammoola. It was from there that I went to Sasimala. She was like a mother to me. So, I told only her about my plans. I told her, 'Don't search for me. I am going to Pulpally to get some land for myself.' And so, I started off. I just took a knife with me; I had no other weapon.

By then Amma was no more. She died when I was studying in Mananthavady. After that I would go to Chirammoola often. Chechi was already married. But I had kept up my relationship with her. I used to go there also. For whatever reason, I always felt closer to chechi than to amma. She had carried me around so much when I was a kid, and I kept this

---
[1] Property owned by the temple administration

love intact even when I grew up. Whenever I got something, I would take it to her. She died of throat cancer, some eight years ago. Till the end, I had a good relationship with chechi. She had two boys.

I went to Sasimala, built a small shed and started living there. There were people nearby. I cleared some forest. Then one day I saw maaman and Munikariyan coming. They had come in search of me, and had searched several places. It was amma's sister who informed them that I had gone to Sasimala. They found me. What else could I do? Where else could I go?

As soon as they came, they said, 'We shall return soon', and took me with them. I had no choice but to obey. It was maaman who was asking me to come, and there was no refusing him. He asked me how much land had I encroached. I said, 'I have taken some land already. I want to clear some more forest and make it my own.' They wouldn't have any of it. I was taken directly to Varghese.

When we reached, Varghese was not there. When he came to know of me being brought, he came the next day. What followed was a full-day counselling session. He stayed at our home and explained so much to me.

He said many things: 'Why do you think a person is born? There are so many events between birth and death that deserve deep thought. These are important questions. We need education. You are now able to read newspapers. That has become possible because you got some education. You know now that we are not the only people here. You know something about this world. You know all that is happening around us. Do you think that the rest of the people have that knowledge? In order to educate your community, you need good education.'

He kept on saying many things like this and more. Finally, I yielded. I gave him my word that from then on I would go to school.

It was at this time that the Thalassery–Pulpally episode took place.² At the time I was in Pulpally, they had this plan in their minds. But I didn't know any of it. As soon as they separated from the party, they were planning all this. Maaman as well as a few other people here knew everything. Many from my place went to participate in the Thalassery attack. After the attack, they all came running back. Maaman was not part of it thinking it was all of no use. But still, it did not affect their friendship. They wouldn't speak to each other about the attack. Varghese, like earlier, used to come to our house and sit there. There was nothing wrong with that. After the Thalassery–Pulpally attack, Varghese came straight to our place. He was in hiding now. Varghese, Ajitha³ and others had led the action in Pulpally. People like Kunnikkal Narayanan⁴ were behind the Thalassery attack. When the Pulpally incident took place, I was right here at home. Varghese had come to maaman's house undercover. Police used to roam around often in our area. How do you think the roads here became good? The roads were repaired

---

[2] The Thalassery–Pulpally episode of 1968–69 was an important event in Kerala's Naxalite movement. Small groups of armed Naxalites, inspired by the Maoist ideology, attacked police stations and landlords in Thalassery and Pulpally. Their aim was to challenge the state and take revenge for the exploitation of Adivasis and landless peasants by landlords and forest contractors. The attack was led by radical youth including Varghese and Kunnikkal Narayanan. The attacks provoked a strong retaliation from the administration, resulting in widespread arrests, deaths and suppression of the movement. Though the armed rebellion was a failure, the episode exposed Kerala's deep agrarian and tribal injustices.

[3] Ajitha, a prominent Kerala Naxalite leader of the 1960s, is now a renowned social activist.

[4] Kunnikkal Narayanan, another important figure of the Naxalite movement in Kerala during the late 1960s, was based in Kozhikode and mobilised radical youth, including his daughter Ajitha.

at the time police were searching for Varghese. Whenever Varghese came to hide in maaman's house, I used to meet him and talk to him.

Once when Varghese was in hiding, he came to maaman's house. They both were now in two different parties. But maaman wouldn't reveal Varghese's whereabouts to anyone. Whatever Varghese asked for, he would ask me to buy it for him. When Varghese came home, he would be fed rice and curry. This was something maaman was very particular about. 'He is moving from place to place. So, he won't get rice and curry everywhere,' so uncle used to tell me, 'If Varghese comes to our house, we have to give him rice and curry for sure.'

Once when he came home, Varghese wanted to go to Panavalli from here. In Panavalli there was one Kuttan Moosath. He was Varghese's friend and Varghese wanted to go to his house. He was hesitant to go alone. He asked me to go with him and drop him off at Moosath's place. I was not at all unwilling to go! But I didn't know the route. I had never crossed this hill to go anywhere. Then Varghese said, 'I can show you the route; you just come with me.' I agreed to that. Maaman also gave his permission. He told Varghese, 'On the way back you just tell him the route and he will come by himself.' Thus, I went with him.

We had to go through the slope on this side of the hill. It was a dense forest. But those days, unlike these days, we didn't have to be scared of going through the forest. There weren't as many wild animals as there are today. Even if a few animals were there, they used to move away when they sensed people approaching. Those days, there were elephants and tigers. When they sensed human presence, they would move to another side of the forest and would never disturb us. We just kept on walking. There was an estate there. A coffee plantation. It was called Pantrung. It was a white man's estate. By the time we reached the estate the sun had risen. We had started early the previous day. Now we could see people on the way. It was difficult to go forward. What if people recognised Varghese? But he was least bothered. He took a shawl and covered his head. He also had a stick in his hand. He just went on walking. No one could recognise him. We went directly to Kuttan Moosath's place. We met him. I was given coffee. I drank it. There was this helper of Kuttan Moosath's. He was instructed to escort me. He took a different route, not the one we had taken while coming. He was told it would be enough to just take me to Thrissilery and I could find my way from there. Thus, I was taken to Thrissilery.

On our way to Panavalli, Varghese and I talked about several things. I asked him questions about Naxalism. That was the first time I asked him such questions. I asked him why he had killed policemen. Then he said, 'They work for landlords and keep us their slaves. So, unless we do away with such people, we won't be able to live here. This land is ours. Earlier it was our land. In the future also, we want to own this land. That's why we had to kill the policemen. But youngsters like you shouldn't jump into situations like this. You have to study now. If your friends ask about all these, don't be scared. You just repeat what all I said to you now.'

I had no knowledge of their split with the party. I was under the impression that they all were communists even now. I didn't know that they belonged to a separate Naxal group.

Thus, I went to study once more. It was in 1969 that I joined school again. That year when I came home for vacation, the Thrissilery episode had happened. I would meet Varghese whenever I came home. Even when he was in hiding, he would come, if he knew I had come home. He would enquire about my studies and marks. He would talk to every single child he came across and ask them about their life.

If the Raavulas and the Adivasis had not been there to help, surely Varghese wouldn't have been able to find his way around the forest. He also could not have gone into hiding here. All around this area, there were landlords. They would have surely betrayed him. He would not have been able to stay on. He could not have done it alone. Adivasis would never reveal anything about him. They would not betray him. Even some landlords had an affinity towards Varghese. They also would not betray him. Even before the Pulpally incident, there were landlords here who liked Varghese. All of them were loyal party workers. That was the basis of the relationship.

16

The Thirunelli–Thrissilery Episode

When the Thrissilery–Thirunelli episode[1] took place, I was home for vacation. In those days, when I came home for vacation, I used to go to work with my friends. In Thrissilery, there is this place called Aanappara where the Adiga was shot dead.[2] Nearby there is a place called Parali. I was working there in one Krishnan's house. My job was to uproot tapioca, cut them into pieces and dry them. For this, I used to get a few coins as wages. With it, I bought my school clothes, set aside some for bus fare, and gave a portion to help with household expenses. When this incident took place, we were at Krishnan's house, slicing tapioca to dry the pieces later. We used to work at night. We would tell each other stories while working. It was then that we heard the sound of gunshot. We thought someone had shot a pig or a rabbit. In those days, people used to go hunting. One could take any kind of gun and go anywhere.

---

[1] The Thrissilery–Thirunelli episode refers to another dramatic phase of the Naxalite movement in Wayanad, during 1968–69. It was closely tied to the Thalassery–Pulpally uprising. Naxalite cadres, led by Varghese, Kunnikkal Narayanan and Ajitha, carried out a wave of attacks. The state responded with severe violence, and encounters, arrests and custodial killings—including that of Varghese in 1970—followed.
[2] Vasudeva Adiga, a landlord, was killed by the Naxalites.

No one would interfere. So, we really thought some pig or rabbit was shot. There was this person called Madhavan amongst us. He said, 'Somewhere a good pig has been shot.' He had a knack for recognising gunshots and identifying what had been fired. We said we could go in the morning and look for the animal. We debated amongst ourselves whether we would get the dead animal or if it would be taken by the hunters.

It was only the next day that we came to know that the shot had been aimed at a human being. Everyone who had heard of the incident was running to the spot. We also went. When the incident happened, people were very frightened.

The Thirunelli–Thrissilery incident happened on the night of 9 February 1970. Under the leadership of Varghese, they attacked houses of six landlords. The landlord of Thrissilery, Vasudeva Adiga, and a businessman from Thirunelli, Chekku, were killed by the Naxals.

The episode unfolded like this. (I got to know all this later from others.) Varghese was accompanied by GROW Vasu,[3] Vellathooval Stephen, Balaraman, Kunhiraman, Vasu, Raghu, Chandran, Rajan, Francis, Narayanan, and Sukumaran. From our community, Choman Mooppan and Batti participated in the action.

On 9 February, the group first went to the house of K. Venkatachala Iyer aka Appuswamy in Thrissilery. They wanted to take a gun from there. The group knocked on the door and entered the house. The people at home were scared. The group asked them to give them the gun, and it was instantly handed over. The group then went to Vasudeva Adiga's place. Adiga was a pawnbroker and had

---

[3] Ayinoor Vasu is a prominent human rights activist, environmental activist and trade unionist in Kerala. He fought for justice for Dalits, tribals and minority communities. He is known widely as GROW Vasu, as he was the founder of GROW (Gwalior Rayon's Workers' Organisation), a union for contract workers.

troubled several people. That was why the Naxals were against him.

When the group reached Adiga's place, they called out to him from outside, and he came to open the door. As soon as the door was opened, they rushed inside the house. The group confiscated all documents related to the pawned property and burnt them. Afterwards they dragged Adiga out. The people who came to the spot on hearing the commotion, ran off as soon as they realised it was the Naxalites. Adiga was shot dead. After that the group went to Paalkadavu in Kulirmavu, to Shoolapaani Warrier's house. They took a gun from there and went to Thirunelli. From there they entered Kesavan Moosath's house. His younger brother Kuttan Moosath was also an accused in the case.

Later on, they reached Chekku's house. Chekku used to run a grocery shop and a tea shop in Thirunelli. The Naxalites killed Chekku, accusing him of being a police informer. At that time, Chekku's son Abdulla was only one and a half years old. But that did not stop them from killing Chekku. The Naxalites had delivered their own verdict and it was carried out.

After the murder of Adiga and Chekku, the group left posters with Naxalite ideology, decisions and slogans. The posters were stuck on the walls of the houses. They also scattered notices explaining the Naxalite action. After the murder the group went into the forest. It was much later that each one of them was caught.

17
After the Attack, Peruman's Murder

There were sixteen members in the group that attacked Adiga. Among the Adivasis were two: Choman Mooppan from Varinilam and Batti from Kaithavally. Both of them passed away. Just like that, six more names from our community were added—and I was on that list. They wanted to include thirty-two accused in the case, following instructions from Adiga's people. They needed to make up the numbers, which is why a few of us were summoned by the police—and we too became accused.

We had voluntarily gone and reported at the station. But they claimed that we were caught from the top of some hill. We had not even heard of that hill. I was the youngest among the people caught.

The people here did not know any of the leaders who took part in that action, except Varghese. The plan for the attack was hatched by GROW Vasu, Vellathooval Stephen, and a few others. This was done from Kozhikode. Not here. They came here from Kozhikode. Eight days after the attack they caught Varghese and shot him dead. It was after this incident that we all were caught. I still remember clearly how Varghese was killed. We didn't witness it. But our people were there. We came to know from them. He hid from the police in a house located slightly above Panavalli. There was one Shivaraman Nair there. Varghese was staying in his house. Everyone said that Varghese had been walking around those areas after the Thrissilery episode. I had not seen him. In fact, I didn't see him at all after the action. People here were of the opinion that he was caught because he had gone to Thirunelli. If he had stayed here in Thrissilery he wouldn't have been caught. Here no one would betray our Peruman. He had gone to Thirunelli to check out the CRP camp. He was really tired after walking for a long time and he slept off in Shivaraman Nair's house. That man betrayed Peruman. And the police came and took him away.

Shivaraman Nair had married a Raavula woman. She also knew about Peruman hiding there. But she never breathed a word. First, Shivaraman Nair went and informed the landlord. The landlord in turn informed the police. Since the police camp was in the vicinity, the news reached the police immediately. That was how he was caught. Even those living nearby came to know of it only when he was being taken away by the police. If they had any inkling of the police coming to the area, police wouldn't have been able to catch Peruman.

The police made Peruman stand in boiling water and poked out his eyes. Even after all this torture, Peruman did not give up the names of others involved in the attack. That's who Varghese was. If it had been someone else in his place, at the very first instance of torture they would have cried out the names of whoever had been involved in the attack. Varghese never even opened his mouth. He was shot dead and the body was taken to the hospital in Mananthavady. We all went there to see him. But the police didn't permit anyone to see him. They were very strict about not showing the body. Not just that, even at the burial place in Vellamunda, no one was allowed to see him.

When we learned of Varghese's death, we couldn't even eat for two days. Not just that, we conducted pela for

Varghese. Many of us were in jail by that time. The money needed to conduct the pela was collected from everyone. If my knowledge is correct, we have not performed pela for anyone not belonging to the community before or after that. Varghese was so much a part of us. If he hadn't been there, there wouldn't have been any change in our lives. After all that he did for us, even the landlords were afraid of doing injustices to us.

We were called by the police saying they would let us go after questioning. But then they needed to make up the numbers. They could not just bring in people from somewhere. So they arrested us. Our names were included in the list of accused. The sub-inspector there at the time was one Muhammad. He knew everything about us. He explained to the crime branch that we were innocent and not connected with the planning or execution of the killings.

He asked the crime branch, 'Why are we putting these people behind bars? They knew nothing about what had happened. They have not even gone to the scene of crime.'

Then IG Lakshmana said, 'You go and do your own work. *We* will take the decisions.'

There was another officer with the crime branch, one Narayanan Nair. He questioned me and I told him everything. He had a friend in our hostel—one Madhavan Nair. Narayanan Nair went to the hostel and enquired about me, to cross-check the truth in what I had told him. From the hostel he got the information that I had gone home for vacation, and that I was expected to return to school. Anyway, after that inquiry, I stopped getting beaten by the police.

Before that, there was this SI from the crime branch. He asked me to lean against the wall and sit with my legs stretched out. And one of the policemen started kicking me on my thighs with his booted feet, while another beat me on the soles of my feet with a cane. Narayanan Nair came in on seeing this punishment. 'What is this? Is it a circus? You shouldn't touch him anymore,' he said to the policemen. And then he turned towards us and said, 'What to do, children—there is no way I can help you. Lakshmana is in charge of this case.'

Later on, when Lakshmana was jailed, we celebrated bursting crackers. He had tortured us so much.

18
To the Jail

We were at first called by the police just for questioning. There was no warrant for arrest. They said, 'We have to ask you a few questions.' Actually, the police took us based on the stories being spread by the people here. There were fabricated stories about us. No one said anything about maaman. He was close to Varghese, but no one mentioned his name. Everyone knew that maaman had not participated in any of these incidents. But I used to speak publicly about my interactions with Varghese and I never concealed my strong admiration for him. I used to say things in public, like landlords should be punished and something should be done to them. Maybe it was because of this that the police took me for interrogation.

First we were taken to Mananthavady sub-jail. But there was no space there to accommodate us. That was why we were shifted to Thalassery and then to Kannur. Even on the way to jail, the police used to beat up the accused. It was like thunder and lightning. A thorough thrashing was mandatory before you were given entry into the jail. The police vehicle which was taking us to the jail was being driven by a friend of mine. He went to the wardens and warned them, 'Don't you dare do anything to these guys. They will not spare you. They will chew you up.' Because of this, the policemen never beat us up on the way. Thus, we were spared the customary police beating before getting into jail. He was the one who saved us.

Even when we were in jail, no one came to beat us. They were afraid because we were jailed in a Naxal case. Moreover, we were tribals. They believed Adivasis were some sort of savages. As soon as we got in, each one of us was given a mat, a pillow, a bedsheet, a plate, a small vessel and a glass. We were taken to the C.P. Block—the closed prison. It would be locked all day. Each cell had one inmate. Prisoners in other blocks were taken out for work. For us even that was not allowed.

Each block used to have a Mesthiri, a supervisor, usually someone undergoing life imprisonment. Our Mesthiri was a man named Rajan. He was undergoing life imprisonment for committing murder. Apparently, he killed a man over some problem, with just a single stab. He would often say, 'If I had known he would die with just one stab, I wouldn't have stabbed at all.'

Rajan took us and put each one of us in the allotted cell. Once inside the cell, you had to wait to step out and see sunlight. The door was opened only once in the morning and once in the evening. We could get out in the morning to have a shower. Then we had to get back in. Rajan used to be our saviour. Every evening the wardens would come and examine all the cells to check if the prisoners had smuggled in something from outside. This was the time when newcomers used to get beaten. Rajan would come to our rescue, telling the wardens, 'Don't get inside, Sir. I have kept them in good humour by supplying them with beedis. If something happens inside the cell, we will not be able to do anything.' Hearing this, the wardens would stand outside at a safe distance. Rajan came inside the cell to check. After the check, he would do the locking up too. So, there was no one to harm us. Rajan used to say, 'These people are not like the ordinary Naxals. They are Adivasis. Don't try to mess with them.' This warning from Rajan kept us safe.

We came to know everyone, and we knew everything that was happening outside. Not even the smallest event outside escaped us. In fact, there were many things we learned inside that people outside might never have heard of. When newspapers came to the jail, they used to censor all news items about Naxalites, by pouring black oil on that part of the paper. They would give us the newspaper only after this. But we would have already learnt about these incidents. We got to know everything. That was one specialty of Kannur Central Jail.

At first, most of us were taken aback by the jail. We knew nothing about the place. And each one of us was given a separate cell. We were not happy about it. At home, we were used to sleeping together in the same place. We were in Mananthavady for ten days. From there we were brought to Kannur. That was how our term of imprisonment as undertrials started. We were sad and upset in the beginning, as we couldn't talk to each other. After a week's time we got used to the situation. The policemen would take us to court, and we always knew our dates. On those mornings, the superintendent would come and ask us to change our clothes. We would take a shower, change into the clothes meant for the trip, and a warden would escort us to the gate. From there, the policemen took charge, and we travelled in their vehicle. The SI from that group would come to the superintendent for permission and we would be taken to the Thalassery court. We were also taken to the Mananthavady and Kannur courts.

Whenever we were brought to Mananthavady, our families came to see us. If they had learned the court date, they would wait for us there. We would request the Magistrate's permission to spend a few moments with them. Then the policemen around would not be able to tell us not to meet them or stop us from talking to them.

The rest of the accused were moved to Kannur, just a month after we were transferred there. In the beginning there were six of us—Marachathan, Chambaran, M. P. Kaalan, Kariyan, Goni and myself. The rest of the accused including Vellathooval Stephen, GROW Vasu, Francis, Narayanan and Gopalan from Valaad, Kuttan Moosath, and Ouseph from Thonikuzhi, came later. The ones arrested for the Pulpally attack were lodged in Kozhikode. After the conviction they were sent to Kannur first. That was when we met them.

19

Memories of the Days Spent in Jail

When we went to jail for the first time, the superintendent there was a man who wouldn't help anyone. I don't remember his name. He was a Pattar from Palakkad. Those days we got only newspapers to read. All newspapers would be there. The others with me did not know how to read. They did not know how to write either. That Pattar superintendent was a morose person. Luckily, after a month of our stay there, he was transferred. When the next superintendent came, we learnt that we could also get books to read. The new superintendent's name was George. He was a good man. As soon as he arrived, he visited all the cells. He talked to us and got acquainted with us. I asked him if I could get anything else to read, apart from the newspapers. That's when I came to know that there was a library in jail, and that we could get books to read from there. He himself asked the warden to show me where the library was.

That was how I started reading books. I started reading just to while away time. There was nothing else to do. I started reading light romantic novels. And I kept on reading more and more of these novels. Once when the superintendent came on his rounds, I was engrossed in reading. He asked me what I was reading. I replied that it was a novel. He then advised me, 'Why don't you use this time to read some books on science, instead of wasting all your time on these novels?' And I decided to give it a try.

After this advice, the first book I read was *From Ganga to Volga* written by Rahul Sankrityayan.[1] This book described life along the river banks. I really enjoyed reading it. It could be read like a story. It also changed my thinking. Because *our* stories about the evolution of man—what I had heard from my community—were quite different. Once I read the scientific facts regarding this, my perspectives started changing. After that, the superintendent would choose books for me and would ask the warden to give them to me. Reading became an intoxication. Meanwhile, the superintendent also asked me to continue my studies. He said he would arrange everything for me. He actually compelled me. But I was reluctant. What do I study now? I refused him, saying that I had lost my interest in studies.

There were also books on Marxism there—Marx's and Engel's books. GROW Vasu had asked for these books for the library. All of them had already read these. But what did I know of such books? That's when the new books came. Vasu gave me a book to read. It was *The Communist Manifesto*. He told me, 'You read this book, comrade. It will change your thoughts and character.'

In jail everyone addressed one another as 'comrade'. When I read this book, I didn't understand a thing. You have to read it twice to make some sense out of it. For those who had some basic knowledge of Marxism, the book would not pose a problem. Such people could learn the book by heart in just one reading. But that wasn't my case. So, I had to read it twice. Vasu and others would have discussions on these books. Once these people arrived in our jail, we were allowed to get out of the cell during the day. We were allowed to walk around inside that block. Vasu started the

---

[1] Referring to *From Volga to Ganga*, the 1943 collection of short-stories by Rahul Sankrityayan.

discussions. There was no ban on such discussions. We had such liberties. When the discussions started, I wanted to study more about Marxism. It is so ironic: I was arrested and made an undertrial prisoner for being a Naxalite and for being part of a revolution, but I came to know of communism and its ideology only during that jail term.

I took out a second book to read—*Mooladhanam*.[2] Again, reading it for the first time, I couldn't understand anything. I read it again. If I had any doubts I would ask Vasu. Vasu would explain it to me. Vasu was a knowledgeable man and an intellectual giant. Only after reading *Mooladhanam* did I understand what socialism was, and what capitalism was. The relationship between the capitalist and the labourer was easy to understand now.

Capitalists and labourers are in two opposing camps, enemies to each other. But for production to happen, they have to come together. I got all this knowledge from jail. After that, they gave me as many books as I could read. I read all of them. Even during that time, I used to be opposed to political killings. Even today my opinion is the same. I don't think any revolution will come about or succeed by killing people. We have to compete with the state. We have to have a democratic fight with them. These were the things I used to say even then. After reading all those books, I started having my own thoughts. And that was how my opinions shaped up.

It was a time of reading and discussions. Whenever I had doubts, I could ask them. I could give my opinions too. Nothing was banned. Things became clearer as we discussed them more. I got to read Nehru's *Discovery of India* and *Letters from a Father to His Daughter*. After reading all these, there was a change in my character. Earlier, I used to get angry the moment someone said something I didn't

---

[2] *Capital: A Critique of Political Economy*, also known as *Capital* or *Das Kapital*, by Karl Marx

approve of. I would use foul language whenever I got angry. All this changed after I started reading.

However, there were a few among us who could not participate in all this. One day, the superintendent asked me, 'These people here from your community are just idling away time. Why don't you teach them how to read and write?' The superintendent got us slates and chalk, and later notebooks and pens. This was a good idea for me also. I could spend my time effectively. And I could teach these Adivasi comrades how to read and write. Once we started teaching and learning, we stopped worrying about home. Anyway, we could not go home now. Then what was the point of worrying about it? This was what everyone thought now.

Around this time, another group of Naxalites, accused of killing someone in Kongad,[3] was also brought to our jail. They had been lodged in Viyoor jail earlier—Ravunni, two college students and another man studying for his LLB degree. I don't remember their names. We formed a group and had a good time together. We would sit together and have various discussions. We would read a book and then discuss it. We should not just believe what others say. We have to read about them and then discuss the ideas. That is how we will get clarity. That was what those comrades were taught. They learnt very fast too. A number of comrades learnt all this in jail—Marachathan, Batti, Goni, Choman Mooppan, Koriyan, M. P. Kaalan, Chambaran. Among the

---

[3] The Kongad Naxal action took place on 30 July 1970 in Kongad, Palakkad district, Kerala, as part of the initial armed activities of the Naxalite movement in the state. In this action, the Naxals captured and beheaded Narayanankutty Nair, a landlord accused by them of exploitation, as a symbolic act meant to instill fear among the landed gentry and inspire peasants to rise. The court found twenty-one people guilty in the case. The main leaders were M. N. Ravunni, Chacko, Bhaskaran, Hamsa and Manikan Nair.

tribals there, I was the only one who knew how to read and write. I first gave them a newspaper to read. And I would ask them what they had understood after reading it. If there were things they couldn't understand, I would explain them. They became very active after reading and writing.

That was how they came to understand the world around them. Next, I gave them story books to read. By the time we got out of jail, all those people had become scholars!

Batti was from Kaithavally. He got interested in the strike for wages because of his adoration for Varghese. When he arrived in jail, he was in a bad state. He had been married recently. He had to leave behind an infant and a pregnant wife. He was very worried about them. I had no such ties to worry about. The only family I had was maaman and grandmother. By the time Batti came out of jail, his wife had remarried. Batti also got married again afterwards.

I still remember the food we were given in jail. In the mornings, we got a sticky, gummy dish made out of wheat, with a little chammanthi[4] to go with it. There was no tea or coffee—only hot water. In the afternoons, we were served two balls of rice. In the evenings, it was one ball of the same rice along with a chapathi. Once a week, we were given fish, and I think it was on Sundays that we got meat.

What we found most difficult was the absence of kanji, which had always been our staple breakfast at home. There was no way to make kanji out of the wheat they gave us—it was far too sticky. We told the superintendent about this, and after that, we began getting chapathi with chammanthi in the mornings instead.

We craved tea or coffee. So, we told the superintendent. He wrote to the jail IG. And it had the desired result. We started getting tea in the morning. Since we were doing things which were helpful to everyone in jail, the other prisoners were so friendly towards us.

---

[4] A coarse paste made by grinding together coconut and dried chillies

20
The Trial

No chargesheet was filed against us, even though we had spent six months in jail. They were not clear about what crime we had committed. But we were regularly being taken to the court. We would go there, get the date for the next appearance and come back. The superintendent used to give some money for our food to the SI accompanying us. But it would never be enough for food, and the SI would always have to pay from his pocket. Poor guy! We spoke to the superintendent and got this practice stopped. From then on, we would take food from jail. For those trips to the court, our food, made in the jail itself, would be ready in packets in the superintendent's room. We collected the packets of food and left.

When the case reached the Mananthavady court, we informed the magistrate that our chargesheets had not been filed yet. When he asked the police about it, they replied that the chargesheet was being prepared and it would be ready soon. Still, we did not get the chargesheet. This was becoming a big problem. We wanted to know what wrong we had done to get arrested and jailed. By then our case was transferred to the Thalassery First Class Magistrate's court. There also, we demanded to see the chargesheet. But that magistrate was least friendly. Moreover, he had a very cold attitude. When the police told him that the chargesheet was being prepared, he would only say, 'Do it quickly.' When we realised that this was not taking us anywhere, we staged a showdown in court demanding our rightful chargesheet. Then the magistrate ordered the police to take us out of the court. We demanded that the police specify an exact date, as to when we would get our chargesheet. We were not ready to move from the court without getting an answer from the police. Police tried dragging us out. We tightly held on to the dock stand. There was a lot of pulling and pushing, at the end of which the dock stand broke. When the magistrate saw this, he hid his face with the paper on which he was writing and fled to his chamber. After this, our case was shifted to the Kannur First Class Magistrate court. Wherever we went, we started demanding the chargesheet. We never had a lawyer to speak on our behalf. Whatever we had to say, we ourselves would say it in court.

Even at Kannur, we kept asking for the chargesheet. The magistrate there was hard of hearing. If we had to say something, we had to go very close to him and shout in the loudest possible voice. Whatever we had to say, it had to be said first-hand. He would not like it if someone else spoke up on our behalf. He was an odd fellow! Anyway, he also said that our chargesheet would be given to us by our next court visit. So, when we went to the court again, after fifteen days, we asked for the chargesheet. And we reminded the magistrate that we had been promised that our chargesheet would be read aloud so that we could hear it. The magistrate then asked the prosecutor where the chargesheet was. He replied that the police had not prepared it yet.

We got to know later what had caused all this delay. There was a dispute going on, as to who would write the chargesheet. There was this SI C. K. Muhammed at the Mananthavady station, who was supposed to prepare it. When he was told to prepare the chargesheet, he said, 'I will prepare a chargesheet purely based on my personal opinion. Most of these people are innocent. We have to exclude them from the case. I can make a chargesheet which clearly states that.'

But the Crime Branch was not ready to take that. If such a chargesheet was filed, it would be equivalent to saying we had been arrested and jailed for no fault of ours. They wouldn't let that happen. They refused to be questioned by Muhammed. They were irritated at the audacity of an ordinary SI questioning them. 'In that case, I will not be part of this chargesheet. You yourselves can prepare it,' said Muhammed SI.

The Crime Branch was in a real fix. They had to submit a chargesheet prepared by the local police. Finally, they decided to meet the CI. He was the one who finally drafted the chargesheet.

It was only when all this was narrated in court that we learnt the power of the magistrate. The man got so angry that he scolded the prosecutor very badly. He used strong words and said if the chargesheet was not submitted by the next hearing, he would let us go free.

The magistrate said, 'It has been six months and more that these people have been in jail. And that too without a chargesheet. Even they do not know what wrong they have done to deserve this punishment.' And he asked the prosecutor, 'How can you keep them in jail anymore?'

Thus, it was this magistrate who got us our chargesheet. By our next visit to the court, there were two copies of the chargesheet ready. One was given to the magistrate, and the other one to us. In fact, each one of us should have been given a copy of the chargesheet. But individual copies were not ready. So, we were given one chargesheet and we read what was written in it. We were happy that at least we had got a chargesheet.

The chargesheet said: we trespassed into a house; we shot one person dead; all of us were guilty of the crime.

The accusation against each one of us was the same. This case went on and on for four years. We had to attend court once every fifteen days or once a month. Even then the case was not posted for trial. Then we started pushing and agitating to hasten that. By then the case was again shifted to the Thalassery sessions court. Till then it had been dealt with in First Class Magistrate courts. But now, it was a judge in place of a magistrate. When it reached the sessions court, we hoped in vain that our case would be posted for trial. Then there was this special prosecutor from the government. In the beginning there was this judge, who soon got transferred.

We decided to go on a strike so that our case would be posted for trial. Earlier GROW Vasu had gone on a month-long hunger strike on this issue. When his condition worsened, the prison authorities escorted him to the hospital, where he was advised to have a glucose drip. But this guy, he would not cooperate. He would just throw away the tubes. At that time Achutha Menon[1] was the Chief Minister. He came to Kannur and went to the hospital where Vasu was admitted, and asked him to stop the hunger strike. He promised that the case would be taken for trial during our next court appearance. Thus, the trial began. By that time, a new judge had taken charge. He was the one hearing the case now. It took around six months for the trial to be concluded.

We did not have any lawyers on our side. Later, one day, M. K. Damodaran[2] came to see us. When he told the superintendent that he wanted to meet us, all of us were summoned. He told us that we had to sign a *vakalat* or *vakalatnama* (advocacy). We wanted to know why we had

---
[1] Chelat Achutha Menon of the CPI served as the fourth Chief Minister of Kerala, from November 1969 to August 1970, and again from October 1970 to 1977.
[2] Former Advocate General (1996–2001) and senior lawyer

to do that. He said he was going to appear for us in court. We told him we had no money to pay the lawyer fees, and so we did not want a lawyer. We could speak for ourselves. By that time, we could recite the entire chargesheet by heart. The lawyer persuaded us, 'You people do not have to give me any money. Just leave the case to me. I will take care of it.' And we agreed and signed the *vakalat*.

Kuttan Moosath, Narayanan and Gopalan had already engaged a lawyer, Kunhanandan. They had spent money also for that. Afterwards, each one of us was given an assistant lawyer. When the trial was to begin, the lawyer said he needed a month's time to study the case in detail. Thus, Damodaran and a few others came to us. They had to see all the locations where the crime had allegedly taken place. They started with Kaithavally. They went there, visited the Pattar's house, met the people there, talked to them, and from there they went to Aanappara. They went to the Adiga's house. From there to Thirunelli, to Chekku's place. They enquired about what had happened. Afterwards, they prepared a map of all these places and episodes. That was to get a clear picture of what had happened that night. Once all this was done, the trial began.

In the beginning, they cross-examined the witnesses. The first witness was a lady from the Pattar's house. She was the wife of Chinnaswamy. She was a very important witness in the case. These Pattars had come from Karnataka. They used to talk in Kannada at home. But whenever they spoke to us, they used Malayalam. When the lady was brought to court, the lawyer said that she did not know Malayalam. If the trial had to happen, there should be someone who knew both Malayalam and Kannada. So, the judge wrote to the court in Kasaragod. A bench clerk who knew both the languages was summoned from Kasaragod. The prosecutor would ask him questions in Malayalam and the bench clerk would then translate it into Kannada for the lady. It took two days to finish that cross-examination. This lady knew Batti and Goni, from among us. They used to go to work at their house.

On the first day, our lawyers asked her the questions. On the second day, it was the turn of Damodaran to ask her questions. At the outset, the lawyer refused help from the translator. Then he asked the lady, 'I had come to your house, and that day you talked to me in Malayalam. Now why are you saying that you do not know Malayalam?' On hearing this, the judge became so angry. Afterwards, all questions to her were asked in Malayalam. There were lots of witnesses in this case. Every one of them was questioned. The case was adjourned for another day. I think the questioning continued for three to four days. Before passing the verdict, the court usually asked the accused if they had anything to say. It was when the judge asked me this question that I read out the declaration I had prepared.

21
A Raavulan's Political Statement

It was *my* decision to prepare a declaration and read it out in court. Everyone supported me. I thought that the seat of justice should know, not just what I had to say, but also what my whole community had to say. I was just an instrument for that. It would be more powerful in the written form. The written word is always sharper! And that proves how important education is for my community.

It was about five pages. This was written down by one of the college students who had come to jail with Ravunni. I cannot remember his name. I dictated it to him, and he wrote it all down for me. Then later on, a fair copy was made. He had such beautiful handwriting! I still remember the beginning of that statement.

> The Indian Penal Code asserts that even if a thousand guilty individuals go free, not a single innocent should be punished. But in our case, if we so much as uproot a stalk of tapioca that we ourselves have worked hard to grow, there is a law to punish us. There are police to arrest us. Yet those responsible for the hunger that kills us go scot-free. When our children die simply because we lack access to medical care, nobody is punished. After all, what law is this, if not bourgeois law?

There are more lines that I remember:

> We have with us a few comrades whose names are unknown to sophisticated society. Ordinary people from the villages as well as those from the cities do not know them. But your rice, your coffee, your pepper, your rubber carry the smell of their sweat and hard work. What makes these valleys fertile are not just the rivers flowing through the Western Ghats, but also the drops of sweat shed by the Adivasis—representatives of tens of thousands of Paniyas, Kurichyas, and Adiyaas. These Adivasis still live centuries behind you. Their slavery is renewed every year at Valliyoorkkavu, and they strictly follow the norms that keep them tied down. This regressive administration is well aware of the brutish treatment meted out to these people by those who continue to exploit them.
>
> Even twenty-five years after Independence, these people are still considered the slaves of independent India. The slavery of yesteryears has been extended to their lifetime. The slavery of today is renewed every year. They remain dependent on the mercy of the master. Perhaps in the earlier days of slavery, they were at least provided for by the landlords. But now, every one of these Adivasis—from men and women to the old and young—must go rummaging for wild tubers on the hillslopes to quench their hunger, even after toiling day and night for the masters. Sometimes, fed up with the wailing of their babies writhing in hunger, they may, under the cover of darkness, cut a banana stalk or a jackfruit, or take some tapioca from the landlords' compound. Though they have given their sweat and blood to grow these, though they have every right to take them in broad daylight, by law they belong to the landlord. We all know what will happen to those who defy these laws. We witness the full cruelty of those in charge of protecting the law. The Adivasi, subjected to the soft caresses of the police and judiciary, may not live further. The police stations in our locality have hundreds of such stories to narrate.
>
> The landlords do not care if these cases reach the courts. For them, what matters is to beat up the trespassing Adivasis.

We know that even in the court of law, the Adivasi has no recourse to justice. Some landlords don't even need the police to mete out punishment—they take direct action using their own henchmen. Those who die as a result of such brutality are declared as deaths by suicide. We have now come to understand that this is how the government and the landlords, in all parts of the country, behave towards the poor Adivasis and agricultural labourers.

You all know very well that our people face the curse of premature deaths caused by starvation and lack of medical facilities. None of these are considered murders. We say this is the cruellest of all murders. Just imagine if we were to file a complaint in the courts of this country, accusing the landlords—who exploit us in the most violent manner—of causing the deaths of our children, who died for lack of medicines or medical care, would such a complaint be accepted by any court or police station?

This is how it went. When the court asked what I had to say, I informed that I had it in writing. I said that I could read it. I read the initial sections and then gave it to the bench clerk. The statement was then read out and handed over to the judge. If I wanted a copy, I had to remit a fee. The prosecutor remitted the fee to get a copy, because he wanted to read what I had written. But I never got a copy. When I came out of jail, I had the full statement in my memory. Now I have forgotten most of it.

The argument in court began only after our side of the story was given. Then started the fight between the lawyers. That was the time we came to know about the map prepared by Damodaran lawyer. The distance from each point to the place where the incident took place, the routes taken through hilly paths, the time to reach Chekku's place, all these were noted down in the map. The map showed that it was impossible for the accused to have walked that entire distance in a single night. No ordinary human could have covered so much ground in so little time. Even the judge could not believe it. So, he was convinced that these were not the only people who had committed the crime; there could be some others involved. The police had not enquired about the others and had just caught these people, putting the blame entirely on them. That was the lawyer's argument. After the arguments concluded, the case was adjourned for pronouncing the verdict. By then the Emergency[1] was declared. The verdict came during the Emergency period. By then it was five and a half years since the incident. On the day of the verdict we did not have to stand in the dock; we were given a bench to sit on.

---

[1] The Emergency in India (1975–77) was a twenty-one-month period marked by suspended civil liberties, press censorship, mass arrests, forced sterilisations and authoritarian rule, provoking deep political and social consequences.

22

Imprisonment under MISA and the Emergency

The court verdict set all the accused free. We were all declared innocent. The court said that the police were yet to catch the real culprits and they had to now catch hold of them. After sometime the lawyer came to give us a copy of the judgement. The prosecutor had made it clear that he would appeal the verdict in the High Court. Though we were set free, we knew very well that we would not be permitted to go home, as it was the Emergency period. We had left the jail in the morning, ensuring that our mats and pillows were kept ready for us. We had even told the superintendent that we would be coming back as we took our leave.

We came out after the verdict. At that time, I had the habit of smoking beedis and cigarettes. When I first went to jail, I did not have this habit. As soon as I got out of the court, I went to a shop to buy a beedi. When I turned back, I saw a policeman following me. He was under the impression that I was trying to run away. He called out, 'Come here, fellow.'

I retorted, 'My job is not to come wherever you call. I have been let free by the court. I do not have to be afraid of anyone now.' My response came out of the confidence given by the verdict.

But the policeman started chasing me. I too ran, and finally went and stood in the court veranda, while he remained outside in the compound. Then the lawyer Damodaran came and told me, 'All your fellow prisoners are in the police vehicle. You too should get in. Anyway, you will be arrested again.'

When I got into the vehicle, I saw all my fellow prisoners there. Another issue cropped up then—the policeman who had chased me wanted to beat me, because I had made him run around.

We were arrested by the Thalassery police. The SI from there told this policeman: 'Remember, these are people who have been in jail for five and a half years, without seeing their homes or relatives. The court has ordered their release. Should they come and stand in front of you asking to be caught? It is your duty to catch them. So what is the point in beating him up?' On hearing this, the policeman no longer wanted to beat me.

From the court, we were first taken to the Thalassery police station. Since there was not enough space to accommodate all of us, we were moved at night to the Koothuparamba station. Altogether, we were thirty-two men. From there, we were brought back to Kannur Central Jail, where we remained until the Emergency was lifted.

We were held under MISA.[1] The case against us was that we had shouted 'Indira Gandhi Murdabad' in the court premises. In fact, we had not done so. It was simply a fabricated reason to put us back in jail. Although it was MISA imprisonment, we still had to appear in court repeatedly. After some time, our status was changed from MISA prisoners to preventive detention prisoners, and we were placed in a special jail created during the Emergency. Here we received certain concessions from the government. We were given monthly allowances, not directly, but sent

---

[1] The Maintenance of Internal Security Act (MISA, 1971) allowed preventive detention, giving the government sweeping powers to arrest without trial. Widely used during the Emergency (1975–77), it became a symbol of authoritarian repression.

to our home addresses. My share was sent punctually to maaman, and that money was of great help to him. As Emergency prisoners, we were not given jail uniforms—not even during trial. In those days, fabric was spun within the jail itself, and our clothes came from there.

The Emergency period was a rotten time. We could hardly bear to see how each prisoner was brought into the jail—it was a terrible sight. Many of them could not even walk properly, as they had undergone the *uruttal* punishment.[2] There was one Velayudhan, arrested in the Thalassery–Pulpally case. He was a Kalari maestro. Our superintendent, a kind man, arranged a special room for him, bought medicinal oils, and allowed Velayudhan to treat those who were badly incapacitated after the punishment. We often went to assist him. I remember some engineering and other college students who were also brought in. They were all fine young men. I even gave them a class on Marx's *Capital*. It was through these youngsters that we came to know about the ill-treatment at the Kakkayam[3] camp—a truly disgusting place.

The only entertainment we had in our first jail term were two packs of playing cards and a chess board. Once

---

[2] The *uruttal* punishment (literally rolling punishment) was a brutal method of torture used during the Emergency in Kerala, particularly reported from the Kakkayam interrogation camp. Prisoners were forced to lie on the ground while policemen rolled heavy wooden logs or poles over their bodies. This caused severe internal injuries, broken bones, and long-lasting physical damage. Many detainees who underwent *uruttal* could barely walk afterwards.

[3] The infamous Kakkayam police camp, a black mark in the history of democratic Kerala, was located in the forest areas of Kakkayam, Kozhikode. This camp was operational during the Emergency period, primarily targeting Naxals. Inhuman and heartless modes of torture were practised here. *Uruttal* was the most notorious of the torture techniques inflicted upon those taken into custody. This camp and the disappearance of Rajan, an engineering student taken into custody, still remain the darkest and most disturbing episodes from the Emergency period in Kerala, or perhaps the entire nation.

we became Emergency prisoners, we could play volleyball. After 4 pm, the superintendent would not remain in his office. He also would come to play with us. Our Mesthiri (Rajan) was also a very good player. By 6 pm the cell doors had to be locked. By that time, we would finish playing, have a shower and get back to our cells. Certain days we extended our game till 6.30 pm. Once we were on preventive detention, our food also was different. We got better food. I have already narrated how we started getting tea during our first term in prison. But the process of dispensing tea became an irritating problem as the days went by. They would bring tea at 5.30 am. They would come and knock at our cell doors. We all would be fast asleep then and used to get really angry at those who disturbed our sleep at that hour. And we had to take the tea at that time. That was the one time of the night we could get some sleep. If we refused the tea, we had to explain why. So it was like, we had to drink it for sure. So still half-asleep, we got up and drank the tea. Once we were under preventive detention all these stopped. We could drink tea when we felt like it.

During the Emergency period, there were people from most political parties in jail. K. G. Marar, who was the leader of Jana Sangh/RSS, along with a few followers, were in our cell. The leaders from the Marxist party were in a different cell. We would not be allowed to mingle with the Marxists. We were thought to be sworn enemies. Naxalites had left the Marxist party due to differences of opinion.

It was during this Emergency period that the appeal in our case was moved. Damodaran was again our lawyer. The prosecutor was one Raghavan Nambiar. We got a favourable verdict from the High Court also. The case was dismissed.

It was during my time in prison that my grandmother passed away. She was very close to me. I got the information about her death. But by the time I came to know, all the rituals were over. So, I didn't go. That remained a huge sorrow in my mind.

23

Freedom, and Activities Afterwards

We came out of jail in 1977, after two more years of imprisonment. So, in total, our prison period had been a solid seven and a half years. When we were about to be released after the Emergency, Crime Branch officers came to the jail. They wanted to know exactly when we would be let out. They said that five or six among us were 'problematic' and that they wanted those people. Their main interest was in GROW Vasu. The superintendent, however, felt that if those five or six were let out with the officers, they might not reach their homes safely. He shared his concerns with us and advised that we wait until dusk to leave the jail. This was no problem for us—after spending seven and a half years in jail, a few more hours didn't make much difference. We were ready to wait. He also instructed us to send word to all party offices about our release.

That evening, we finally got our liberty. Everything looked strange to us, and we didn't even know which way to go. When I say 'we', I mean a group of eight people from Thrissilery. Somehow, with much difficulty, we reached the bus stand. Those days were very different from now—after sundown, the town would be completely deserted. And since it was night, there were no buses to Mananthavady. The only place we knew was the police station; so we went there and met the SI. He allowed us to stay there for the night. The next morning, a policeman came with us and helped us board a bus to Mananthavady. Since we had been given an allowance from the jail, we were able to use it for the bus fare and food.

When we reached Mananthavady, the place felt even stranger. We were like hens left out on a moonlit night—completely disoriented, unable to figure out which direction to take. Everything was unfamiliar, yet we had one goal: Thrissilery. We decided to walk, relying on our memory from years ago. Eventually, we reached Motta (Ondayangadi), and from there moved on to Varinilam. The whole place had changed. Little children who saw us did not recognise us, but the older women along the way could. They spoke to us, curious to hear our stories. Finally, I reached home. By then, maaman had shifted to a new place. The earlier house—which was on land owned by me—had been sold by him while I was in jail. He sold it to raise money for my grandmother's death rituals. Much earlier, he had sought my opinion about selling it, and I had not agreed. It is never easy to sell a property belonging to someone in jail; my uncle had to go to great lengths and face many difficulties to complete the sale. I felt deep sadness for having stopped him when he first asked. It was only after my return that the formalities for officially changing the ownership in the papers were completed.

As soon as we arrived, people came rushing to see us. We were the first from that place to have gone to jail, and everyone was curious. It felt as if we were beings from another planet. We had a little money that would last us a few days, but we had no work at all. Just because we played volleyball in jail, we hadn't died of excess bile. At first, it was very difficult for us to work, and most people were reluctant to offer us any work. The first to call us was Appasamy from Kaithavally. It was from his house that the Naxalites had taken the gun. I was totally unable to work at first.

I had been sent to jail while still going to school. It was my comrades in jail who taught me how to work, and in return, I taught them how to read and write. They showed me how to build ridges in the fields. Once I started working, I began forming good relations with the people there, including the Marxists. They invited me to join the party.

All of us, except Choman Mooppan, joined the party. We had all learned Marxism in jail. However, Mooppan had, from the beginning, believed in Naxalism. I used to argue with him in jail that their ideology of complete destruction was foolish. Even after he returned, his views remained unchanged. I believed CPM was the better option; so I joined them.

I gained recognition in the party after a study class. Two people, Raghavan Warrier and Krishnan Warrier, regularly took classes, but they were not very knowledgeable. Once, during a class at Kaattikulam about Marx's *Capital*, I asked a question they could not answer. I spoke up, sharing all that I knew, and after that, people in the party began to respect me. That is how I got my membership. Maaman was also an active party worker at the time.

After returning from jail, people gave me respect. If there were problems, they would come to me, and we would be at the forefront of resolving them. We conducted a few strikes, including the *pathambu*[1] strike and the strike for wages. In those days, the system was called 'harvesting for

---

[1] In the Central Travancore region and Wayanad, agricultural labourers were traditionally paid through a system called *pathambu*, also known as *patham*. After the harvest and threshing, when the crop was measured, a labourer was entitled to one *para* of paddy for every 7, 8, or 9 *paras* of total paddy, depending on the arrangement. This portion represented their wages. However, most of the time, labourers were denied the paddy that was rightfully theirs. During the *pathambu* strike, agricultural workers protested to claim the full measure of paddy due to them under this prevailing system.

pathambu'. If we harvested seven *paras*, the next para was meant for the labourer. But landowners refused to honour this. We staged the *pathambu* strike to assert this right. The strike for wages started when our wages were withheld. It was significant because it was led by agricultural labourers against landlords who were part of the same communist party. They threatened that the strike would be futile. But we persisted—if we worked in their fields, we deserved to be paid properly, both in wages and paddy. Leaders from Kannur intervened, as the Mananthavady party was under the Kannur district committee. After discussions, it was resolved to give wages in money rather than paddy. The landlords agreed, and other landlords followed suit. C. M. Gulikan, his elder brother Jogi, Vijayan, and others worked for the Adivasis here.

24
Work, Family

After trying out several jobs, I finally took up sawing wood, which paid slightly better wages. During this period, I got married. Her name was Kaali, and she belonged to my community. We married following all the traditional rituals. However, I did not follow the custom of bearing all expenses at her place for one year. We were together for five years. Then we separated. Every time she became pregnant, she had a miscarriage in the third month. I took her to Dr Mercykuttiamma in Mananthavady, who prescribed one injection every month and insisted that she take her medicines without fail. I would buy the medicines for her, but she never took them. I grew very angry, as I had been setting aside money from my wages to buy the medicines. I had hoped very much to have children. That ultimately led to the breakdown of our relationship. As per custom, after the divorce, I bought her all the things—sari, bangles, etc. I also gave money to her relatives.

After this, I married Sarojini from another caste. It was in 1981. That was the period when I used to go for sawing wood. I had gone to Shankaran Master's house to saw wood when I first saw her. She did not have many relatives or family. Her mother had abandoned the family when Sarojini was very young. She had a sister who was adopted by someone. Sarojini at that time was living with an acquaintance's family in Thrissilery. She used to go to work from there. The proposal came from the lady she was living with. Sarojini was also willing to marry me. That is how our wedding took place. Since we were from two different communities, we had our wedding at the registrar's office. Maaman himself conducted the wedding at the Mananthavady Registrar Office. After the wedding, we started living in Varinilam, near maaman's house.

If we marry from another community, there are a few rituals to be conducted, in order to bring the spouse into the Raavula community. We had to give *thappu vala*[1] to the elders as penalty. The number of *valas* (bangles) is decided as per the gravity of the wrongdoing. It would change from time to time. Nowadays, instead of *valas*, you have to pay money.

The structure of the Raavula community is based on three 'Mantus'. These three Mantus are Thirunelli, Potharu and Bedaak. Each Mantu has its own headman. They are known as Mantileyan. Under each Mantu there will be five to ten 'Chemmangal'. One may roughly equate a Chemmam to a family. Children will belong to their mothers' Chemmam. Matriliny is important to our community. Relations are decided by Chemmam. When we marry, we should not marry from our own Chemmam. Therefore, if we marry from other communities, when they are being brought into our community, they will not be able to join the partner's Chemmam. They will have to get adopted by an elder from

---

[1] *Thappu vala* is a penalty offered to the ancestors and deities as a compensation for the wrongs and offenses committed, knowingly or unknowingly, in one's day-to-day life. The penalty is given in the form of *valas* (bangles) made of brass. Depending on the severity and nature of the wrongs or deviance committed, the number of *valas* would vary. Sixteen is the highest number and usually the number is fixed in proportion to the wrong done or the seriousness of the deviance.

another Chemmam. My wife Sarojini was made part of the Paneli Chemmam. My Chemmam is Kaalangottu.

My eldest daughter, Saritha, was born in 1982. I loved children, and she felt like a precious gift after a long wait. But she died young, which was a huge shock for me. I had to go through a very difficult time to cope with the loss. One night she became sick, and by the time she was hospitalised, she had passed away. She was only four years old. It happened on 1 June 1986. We had even purchased a bag and dress for her school admission, but she never got to use them.

In 1985, my son Sarith was born. He later completed a hotel management course and worked for some time at the Aashramam School. He married a girl from the Paniya community. When he was studying at Thrissilery Government High School, I served as the PTA President there.

Over the years, I have held several leadership roles in my community, including President of the Thrissilery Scheduled Tribe Cooperative Society, the Appapara Girijan Society, and the Thrissilery Handloom Society, among others. The one that remains clearest in my memory is my work with the Handloom Society.

It was around 1985 or 1986 that the Handloom Society's activities began. Started with government aid, it was the first Handloom Society in Thrissilery. They built a facility, provided training in spinning and weaving, and only then began production. The threads and other materials were brought from Kannur, and the finished clothes were also sent there. Initially, it functioned well. But after five or six years, problems started, and the society had to be closed. Now the building, looms, and wooden articles are decaying. If it had continued properly, it could have been a successful institution.

I also served as a Panchayat member, representing the Thrissilery ward from 2005 to 2010. I was an active CPM member, as was maaman before me. One unique feature of Thirunelli Panchayat was that, since its formation, it had always been administered by the Left. During my tenure as Panchayat member, I also served as the Standing Committee Chairman for Scheduled Castes and Scheduled Tribes.

25

I Start Learning about My Community

By the time I returned from jail, maaman had become an important Mooppan here. But I was under the belief that all these were superstitions and irrational practices. I never used to participate in any community functions. I wanted to eradicate all these practices with maaman on the forefront of such an effort.

Gradually I started attending community functions. After a while, I began accompanying maaman and started learning everything. By this time, maaman had started performing Gaddika on public stages. He had his first programme in Trivandrum. People had started hearing about Gaddika by that time.

Meanwhile, one Rameshan came to maaman, asking for help to learn about our community. He needed this for his research. If my memory is right, this was in 1998. The very first person to study the Raavula community in detail was this Rameshan Master. Now he teaches at Mananthavady Government College. The friendship we began at that time continues even today.

Back then, maaman was too busy with many things; so he handed over this Rameshan Master to me. He wanted to learn everything I knew about the Raavula community. But honestly, what did I know then? I had no real knowledge to share with him. The truth is, I was learning about my own community along with Rameshan Master. To gather knowledge, we travelled together to Karnataka and to several places in Wayanad where the Raavulas lived. Those travels, and my time with Rameshan Master, changed me a lot. I too began to learn so much about my community. In fact, it was only then that I truly came to understand my community.

It is only in Kerala that we are called Adiyaas or slaves. In Karnataka our people are known as 'Yeravar'. In the Coorg district of Karnataka, there are a lot of Raavulas. There are many of them living in the outskirts of the Beechanahalli dam. Both the Raavulas in Wayanad and the Yeravars of Karnataka speak the same language. Even today both groups keep in touch for many matters. Thus, it was through these travels that I learnt a lot of things about the origins of the Raavulas.

Thus, I was able to tell K. Panoor, who is celebrated by many as the scholar who wrote about Adivasis, that whatever he had written was nonsense. He doesn't know anything about Adivasis. I had read his book *The Africa of Kerala*.[1] The whole book is rubbish. I had told him this to his face. I told him it was all wrong. In fact, when I read this book, I got really irritated. So, I never read any of his other books. He had worked here as Tribal Officer. He had no other connections. He wrote what he had come to believe. He did not study deeply about Adivasis. In fact, a good book about our life is yet to be written.

---

[1] *Keralathile Africa* (The Africa of Kerala) is a controversial work by K. Panoor. A travelogue, it was published in 1963. It described the miserable condition of tribals in the Wayanad region. The book caused quite a stir and a debate in the Kerala Legislative Assembly about the conditions of the Adivasis. It has come to be seen as an important document for tribal studies.

I got into full-time community work after maaman's death. He passed away on 11 November 2007, due to cardiac arrest. The emptiness that his absence left in my life was no small matter. My maaman was my guide, my guru, my strength, and the light of my life. Our bond was not only because he had looked after me from childhood, but also because I had never done anything in my life without consulting him. Ours is a matrilineal community, and maaman was everything for me. For me, maaman was the be-all and end-all. It took me a long time to adapt to a life without him. Later, I began to take initiatives for the community. I started performing Gaddika on public stages, leading community matters, and sharing what I had learned with others. By then, I had mastered all the songs and rituals.

After that, I stopped doing wage work. Community matters became my priority. I shared knowledge with anyone who wanted to learn about us. I participated in workshops, taught the younger generations the songs and Gaddika, and dedicated myself fully to our traditions. By this time, my thinking had also changed. I realised that what we had were not irrational practices, but living traditions worth protecting. For that, documentation was necessary. Even now, I am trying to write my community into history. We should not lose anything. That is why I am deeply interested in narrating as much as I can about my people.

26
The End of the Story of Our Origins

———•••●•••———

The Raavulas are one of the most important tribal groups in Wayanad. Alongside us, the other prominent tribal communities here are the Paniya, Kurichya, Mullukuruma, Vettakuruma, Kaattunayka, Thachanaadan Mooppan, and Wayanadan Kaadar. Although our community's real name is Raavula, we are more commonly known as Adiya. I will tell you how this came to be. But before that, let me finish the story of the origins of the Raavulas.

***

Maali was kept waiting outside while Paakkathappan went in. He bathed, and had his food. He also gave food to the two humans who were hiding there. He rested for a long time. All this while Maali was eagerly waiting for her prey. She sat there gazing around. In front of the fort, a beautiful river flowed. On the other three sides stretched a thick forest. A cool breeze blew, and the whole atmosphere was soothing. Maali was sitting there all engrossed in the beauty of the place when Paakkathappan came apologising to her for making her wait.

He said to her, 'Just think about it. You have devoured all of God's creations. Now only two of them are left. If you eat them up today itself, what will you do tomorrow when you are hungry?'

That question made Maali think. She realised her blunder. 'What will I do when I am hungry tomorrow?' She asked Paakkathappan, 'What do you think is the solution?'

Paakkathappan said, 'You let those two go free. A race of humans will arise from them. And they will give you your food.'

Maali wanted to know how that would come about. Paakkathappan continued,

'Transform yourself into the shape of a common lizard or a rat. You should hide among the dry leaves in the humans' path. When they approach, you have to scare them by making a *krr krr* sound. You will not be able to kill them. But you can scare them. Out of fear, they will fall sick. Then, to appease you, they will beat their drums, sing, and offer you pieces of coconut. From that day, your original form will be lost forever.'

Maali agreed to this. Thus, the two humans got their lives back. They were Ithiyachan and Ithiyamma. They were our ancestors. It was from them that everything came into being.

27

Rituals and Customs of the Raavulas

The Raavula home is called Kullu. If there are more shacks in one area, they are together called Kuntu. Each Kuntu has a Mooppan. He is known as Kuntukaran. The Mooppan is chosen from among the knowledgeable elders. All the rituals in the Raavula society are conducted under the leadership of the Naatukaran, Kuntukaran and Chemmakaran. If it is a religious ritual, it would be led by the Kanalaadi, Karimi and Thammadikkaaran. The main gods of the Raavulas are Karingaali, Malakkaari, Kuliyan, Paakkathappan and Maariyamma.

As I said in the beginning, we have lots of songs. We have different songs to go with each ritual. These songs, always accompanied by the rhythm of the drum and the melody of the blowpipe, are also stories. These stories are a mixture of history and myths.

Since we came from Karnataka, our language has much similarity with Kannada. The Raavula language is a blend of Kannada and Malayalam. All our songs are in this language. It has no script of its own. So, these songs were passed down orally for generations. Now they are being preserved in writing, using the Malayalam script, so that the younger generation can learn them.

In all Raavula rituals, music and musical instruments hold a central place. The most important among them are the *thudi* (drum) and the *cheeni* (pipe). The *thudi* is made by carving out a block of wood, with both ends covered in animal skin. A special drumstick is used to strike it, and when tapped in rhythm on the stretched skin, it produces the sound. The *cheeni* is a perforated wind instrument. Two palm leaves are tied together at one end of the instrument, leaving a small gap. When air is blown through this gap, the music emerges.

Our community has many rituals that are to be observed in each stage of an individual's life—from the embryo stage until death. When a pregnant woman completes eight months, a ritual called Peyattu is performed to drive away evil spirits and ensure the wellbeing of the newborn. To ease childbirth, another ritual called Arangattu Baangal is conducted by the Naatukaran. After birth, the next important ritual takes place on the twenty-eighth day, when a thread is tied around the baby's waist.

When girls attain puberty, a ritual called Manjal Neeru is performed. The girl is made to stay in a separate part of the house and is not allowed to go out during this time. The ritual itself resembles a mini wedding. Manjal Neeru is conducted at night and continues till the next morning, with singing and dancing. Around 11 am, the older women take the girl for a ritual bath. After the bath, she is dressed in a sari. Once Manjal Neeru is completed, it signifies that the Raavula girl is ready for marriage.

Weddings take place at the bride's house, with celebrations held at night. Drums and songs are mandatory. In earlier days, there was a custom called Kolubelli (*'kolu'* means firewood and *'belli'* means paddy). Once the wedding was fixed, the groom had to bring all necessary items to the bride's house, including rice and firewood. This custom is no longer followed. At weddings, the groom must give money to the bride. Marriage within the same Chemmam or family is not allowed; one must marry outside. The Naatukaran leads the ceremony, accepting *valas* (ceremonial bangles) from both families before starting the rituals. Wedding songs are sung, praising the bride's abilities and her ancestors' fame. Widows were allowed to remarry, but with one condition: the money given by the first husband during the first wedding had to be returned to his family.

When a death happens, it is first informed to the Kuntukaran. He arranges for a Karimi to pass the news to relatives. The remaining rituals are done by the Karimi. The dead body is bathed in hot water. After the bath, if it is a woman, the body is covered with a sari. If it is a man, his head is tonsured, smeared with sandal paste, and then the body is covered with a white cloth.

The body is laid in the courtyard with the head facing south. The Naatukaran and Kanalaadi perform the rituals. If the deceased had committed any wrong in life, the relatives had to pay a fine in the form of *thappu vala*. After the rituals, the body is taken to the cemetery. It is placed on a bamboo cot, and on each of the four corners, a coin is kept. Another coin is placed near the head before closing the pit. The grave is then covered with soil, and brambles are laid on top—this is to prevent the soul from entering another body. The soul is entrusted to Chudala Bhadrakaali before the Karimi and his group return from the cemetery. Later, a pela is conducted to entrust the soul to the elders.

There are two types of pela—Cheriya (small) Pela and Valiya (big) Pela. In the Cheriya Pela, the Karimi goes to the cemetery with food and offerings for Bhadrakaali. He extracts the soul from there and hands it over to the family elders. A Valiya Pela is also known as Koottam. Here, the Karimi, covering himself with a blanket, performs rituals to invoke the soul, which possesses him. The headman then asks questions, and the soul replies. To send the soul away, the Karimi cross-dresses as a woman and ties a brass plate to the sari. The soul, now ready to depart, obeys the Naatukaran's guidance. Before leaving, the soul blesses everyone present. Finally, the brass plate is untied, marking its journey to the other world.

28
Gaddika—for Humans and Nature

It was Ithiyachan who invented Gaddika. To put it simply, Gaddika is performed for humans as well as nature. Another important ritual is Thera. Thera is conducted once in a year. There are separate songs for Thera. One ser paddy, coconut, plantain leaf, broken rice, etc., will be kept before a lit Nilavilakku (lamp). This ritual is conducted by the Karimi. Songs are sung in front of the lamp. It begins at night and continues till dawn.

Gaddika is of three types—the Gaddika performed when someone is unwell, Poojagaddika and Naattugaddika. For the first kind, only one measure of rice and one coconut are needed. This is done when a person is sick, or when someone gets frightened and becomes speechless. It is performed either in the house of the sick person or in a relative's house. Through this ritual, the reason for the illness is revealed. No wages should be demanded for this performance.

If the person recovers, as a token of gratitude to the deity believed to have cured the illness, Poojagaddika is performed. For this, offerings like silk cloth, flattened rice, fried paddy, bananas, a rooster, coconut, rice, paddy, and ragi are placed before the lit Nilavilakku.

The third type, Naattugaddika, is performed for the naadu—one's place or region. If the other two are for individuals, this is done for the land where people live. It is performed to exorcise the evil spirits that have entered the place, and it is supposed to bring goodness to the land. It also has the name Naaduneekkal, which means clearing off a place. It is Lord Shiva's lieutenant gods who cause illness. This Gaddika aims at deporting them from the place. Gaddika is performed for each area. Goddess Maariyamma is summoned. It is Maariyamma who has the power to deport the petty gods under Lord Shiva.

During Naattugaddika, men dress up as Maariyamma, wearing women's clothes. They divide themselves into two or three groups and go from house to house in the area, taking offerings for the deity. At the end, all the groups come together in one place to complete the rituals. Unlike the other forms, Naattugaddika has more dialogues than songs.

29
How the Raavulas became Adiyaas

How did the Raavula become Adiya is a topic that needs to be discussed deeply. In Karnataka they are still called Yeravar. So how did they become Adiya in Kerala?

The Raavulas like travelling a lot. Centuries ago, our ancestors never stayed put in one place—they kept on wandering. Maybe because of this, they are known as Yeravars in Karnataka. 'Yeravar' means wanderers. These people with wanderlust kept travelling, crossing borderless forests, and finally reached Wayanad. Centuries ago, it was deep forest all around. In those days, Wayanad was ruled by hunter kings. As per their order, the Raavulas became agriculturalists. In the beginning, they cultivated ragi and millet. They would set fire to small shrubby patches inside the forest and start cultivating there. Later on, they cleared marshy areas of the forest and turned them into fields for paddy cultivation. They built temples and kaavus and worshiped many gods. They lived in small huts.

As time went on, Brahmins reached Wayanad. They became the priests in the temples where the hunters and tribals worshiped. They chanted mantras in a language unknown to the tribals and conducted their poojas. They deceived these innocent tribals, saying theirs was god's language and that they were god's representatives on the earth. They brought in the Warriers and Maaraars to assist them. They made people believe that the earth and sky belonged to the gods, and therefore, whatever is on this earth belonged to the gods inside the temple. The tribals, who deeply believed in gods, also believed what the Brahmins told them. They devoted everything that came out of their hard work to the gods. Gradually, these temple residents became the owners of the land. And we, the original claimants, became the Adiyaas of this earth. This is how the Raavulas turned into Adiyaas. Those temple residents became the lords, and the Raavulas became Adiyaas—slaves.

This history keeps repeating. The Raavulas had to live under whomsoever became the owners of the land, as Adiyaas, through generations. On the very earth that rightfully belonged to them, they did slave's work and ended their lives, generation after generation.

Even now, though tribals have been freed from the landlords, they still remain slaves to governmental organisations, spending their lives waiting endlessly for an administrator's sympathy.

Even our original name, Raavulan, has been snatched away from us. This has to change. The basis for this change is surely our own culture, our own history. It has to be documented properly. I am doing what I can to bring about that change. The youngsters of the new generation should take over from us.

Tomorrow, the world should know that a people, a community, and a culture once lived here. Every history is precious.

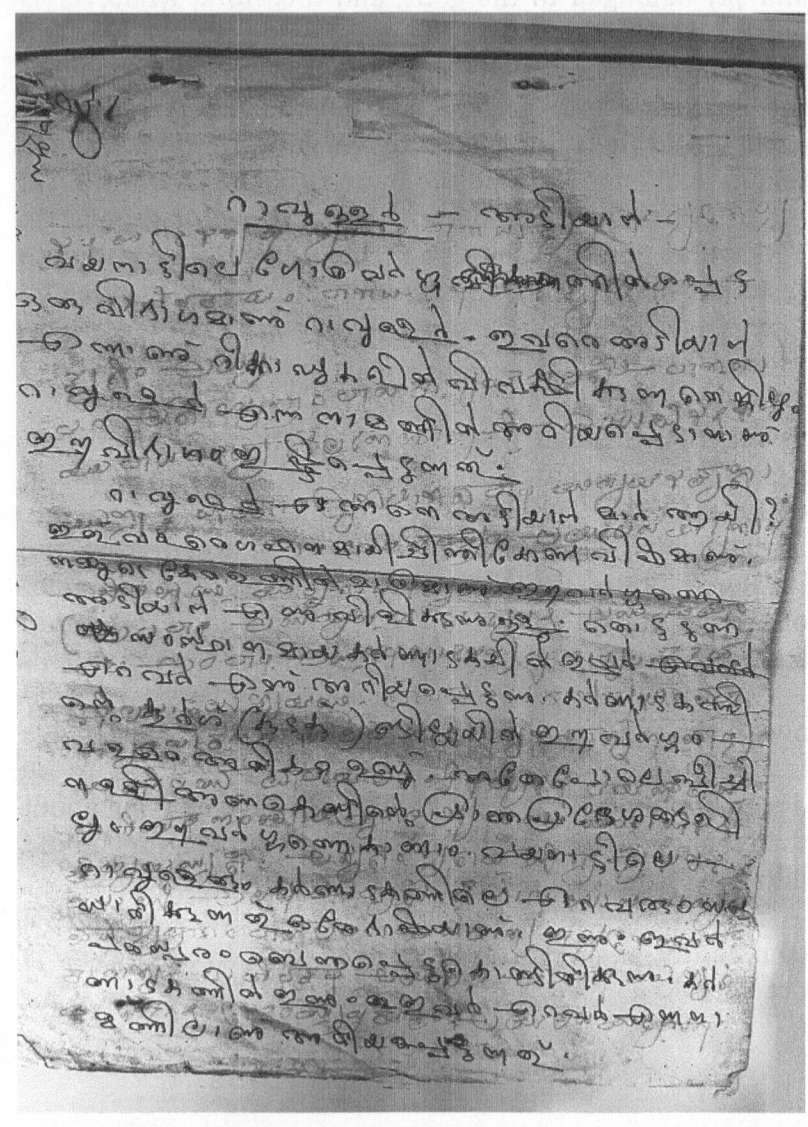

Handwritten notes by Kariyan tracing how the Raavulas came to be known as 'Adiyaas'.

Postscript

Kariyan Mooppan left this earth on 10 March 2020, after a long, hard fight against cancer. When I went to Kaithavally that day to see Kariyettan for one last time, I had the vision of an eighty-one-year-old man climbing those narrow steps to that house. I imagined the old man, his revolutionary zeal still alive despite the age, clenching his fist above his head, shouting slogans. If that man, who fought for the Adivasi in Thirunelli and Thrissilery and the entire Wayanad, was alive, he would have surely come to the last rites of that high-school student who was inspired by the same struggle. Or shall I say, if he had not been killed fifty years ago, rather than saying if he was still alive? The former perhaps does justice to the man. Just as the Thirunelli–Thrissilery episode of 1970 terminated the life of the revolutionary A. Varghese, it transformed the life of that student, P. K. Kariyan.

I often think about what might have happened to Kariyettan's life if he had not been made an accused in a case he was not even part of. Perhaps he would have continued his studies at Kalpetta S.K.M.J. High School. As his dear comrade had advised, he could have become well-educated and worked for the uplift of the Raavula community. Yet, though Kariyettan could not continue his education, he lived and worked for his community. He was always alert and active in spreading Gaddika and knowledge about the Raavulas.

For me, Kariyan Mooppan is—first and foremost—the rhythms and harmony of his voice. He told me his life, pausing at times, summarising at others, his feelings melting seamlessly into his voice.

I think the clarity in his speech came both from his education and from his life in jail. These two experiences gave him deep insights and were instrumental in shaping the person he became. Once, when I asked him if he had ever been disappointed about not completing his studies, he just smiled, offering no answer. Perhaps he was quietly touched by that sorrow. His maaman, P. K. Kaalan, had wished that his sister's son, Kariyan, should study well. Kariyettan always remembered, with deep feeling, how his uncle had gone out of his way to create opportunities for his education.

Kariyan Mooppan at his home in Wayanad

He firmly believed that a leader should be like a fish in water among his people. Kariyettan's politics emphasised that without the people, there can be no true people's vanguard. He often said that it was the armed revolutions in Varghese's time that brought about real change to the lives of Adivasis—improving wages, ensuring basic human treatment of the tribals, and providing essential facilities like transport. But today's revolutions in the forest, Kariyettan felt, cannot change the day-to-day life of Adivasis. Those who seek societal change must work among the people. He held this belief steadfastly until the end of his life.

Now only his words remain. But those words have a historical role. This is the life of one of the earliest Adivasi–Naxalite political prisoners from Kerala. His words capture—both culturally and organically—the life of one of Kerala's most significant tribal communities, the Raavulas. And there is nothing more gratifying than to have been the transcriber of these words.

It is easy to narrate stories about those who are dead. But to narrate life itself is not easy. When I first stepped into his Kaithavally house, to talk about writing about his life, he was healthy. But by the time he started narrating his life, cancer cells had started spreading though his body—though he was unaware of it. With each subsequent meeting, I noticed his excitement waning and his voice growing tired. The last time I met him at the Mananthavady District Hospital, sitting near him and waiting for each word, I felt guilty. Why had I delayed so long in telling this life? Was I causing more pain to a man already suffering? I resolved to wait until he recovered, to meet him and continue the narration. But the illness snatched him away.

It took another two years for this book to come together. I have no justification for this delay, and I sincerely apologise to Kariyettan. Those two years were also pandemic years. Once I overcame the struggles of the pandemic, it was Kariyettan's son Sarith who helped me resume from where Kariyettan had left off. In that leaky house, he had, like a treasure, preserved Kariyettan's handwritten notes and other documents. Without those notes, I would not have been able to complete this work. I also remember with gratitude Kariyettan's wife, Sarojini. Heartfelt thanks also to my dearest friend Chitra Elizabeth, a fellow traveller through the various stages of this book; to R. K. Bijuraj, Chief Subeditor at *Madhyamam*, who shared valuable suggestions and documents; and to P. Hareendran, Head of the Rural and Tribal Sociology Department, Kannur University, Mananthavady Campus; and Baiju Koduvally, Senior News Photographer, *Madhyamam Daily*, for providing Kariyettan's photographs. I also thank Mathrubhumi Books for publishing this book in Malayalam.

From the moment I decided to write the life story of Kariyan Mooppan, my partner Saheed Rumi walked with me throughout this journey. My love and gratitude to my umma, P. K. Kadeeja, who always motivated me to write; my bappa, T. A. Abdulla; and my siblings, Fasna and Faizal. Without all of you, this book could not have been completed.

Kariyettan now rests in the soil of Thrissilery, in the valley of Brahmagiri, where history and revolution are interwoven. As the Raavulas believe, he remains ever-present in that land, alongside all his ancestors.

As they say, none of those who are dead ever truly leave this earth.

Fazeela Mehar

Fazeela Mehar is a writer and journalist from Wayanad, Kerala. She has been part of the editorial teams at *Madhyamam Daily*, *Mathrubhumi Daily* and *Manorama Online*. Her debut novel *Khanithath* was shortlisted for the D. C. Books Novel Award in 2018 and the Kendra Sahitya Akademi Yuva Puraskar in 2024. She received the K. A. Kodungalloor Award in 2022 for the best short story in Malayalam.

V. Prathiba retired as Associate Professor of English Language and Literature from the University of Calicut, Kerala, concluding a distinguished teaching career of thirty-seven years. A firm believer in the power of meaningful dialogue to address historical oppression, she uses translation as a way to engage with voices of disadvantaged groups. She co-edited *The Oxford India Anthology of Malayalam Dalit Writing*, and her forthcoming translation, *My Life*, is the autobiography of environmentalist Kallen Pokkudan. She currently resides in a senior living community in Bengaluru.

P. Sanal Mohan is a distinguished historian and former Professor in the School of Social Sciences at Mahatma Gandhi University, Kottayam, Kerala. He has held fellowships and academic assignments in universities in India and abroad. His work engages with caste, religion and modernity. He is the author of *Modernity of Slavery: Struggles Against Caste Inequality in Colonial Kerala*, a seminal study that explores the lives of salve castes and the emergence of Dalit consciousness in nineteenth-century Kerala. His areas of interest include colonial modernity, social movements, questions of identity, Dalit movements and Christianity in India.